ANOTHER LOOK:
Growing up in The Jim Crow South

Another Look:

Growing up in The Jim Crow South

By: Betsy Bunn

Illustrations By: Meg Abbey

inkind Design

Inkind Design - The Kinder Design Solution
www.inkind-design.com
2015

First Printing: 2015

ISBN <978-0-692-59831-3>

Inkind Design
www.inkind-design.com
meg@inkind-design.com

Illustrations by Margaret E. Abbey

Ordering Information:
Special discounts are available on quantity purchases by corporations, associations, educators, and others. For details, contact the publisher with the above listed contact information.

U.S. trade bookstores and wholesalers: Please contact Inkind Design
Tel: (508) 328-5000 or email meg@inkind-design.com.

THIS BOOK IS DEDICATED
TO MY BELOVED HUSBAND FRANK BUNN
AND TO ALL OF MY FAMILY
PAST AND PRESENT
WITH GRATITUDE
FOR THEIR LOVING AND PATIENT PRESENCE
IN MY LIFE

A Young Betsy Holland

FURTHER THANKS TO THE FOLLOWING PEOPLE

Kendall Dudley for his wisdom, guidance and patience
during the gathering of this book

Bill Blaine Wallace for his willingness and keen perception
in writing the introduction

Kathy Roberts for her skilled proofreading and keen insights

Mopsy Strange Kennedy, Louise Cochran, and Olivia Hoblitzelle
for reading advance copy and writing commentary

Gail Abbey for careful reading and feedback

Foreword

Introduction

The Jim Crow South

Stories, Mostly Southern, Past and Thereafter

Essays

Epilogue

A Photographic History

Foreword

"It's not nice to stare." I'm grateful this larger than region manner was of no mind to Mrs. Godard, Betsy's mom, at least as Betsy remembers her mom through the pages of this beautiful book.

Betsy stared, still stares---*I slip off to my little room to catch up on my staring, a practice I developed years ago. Just looking out the window and not thinking is more restorative than sleeping or reading.*

Betsy's is a generative stare, no nosey gaze, effortlessly passing muster in a region more mannered than most. No staring at people. Betsy watches the spaces between people, between people and places and things. Eyes wide, Betsy's gaze is respectfully convivial. Her attention is to the relational moment.

I call that prayer. Betsy reminds me that prayer is awareness of the immediate. Nothing lofty about that. Betsy's book is an earthy blessing.

Betsy reports way before she appraises. Words left alone, not dissected and interpreted, are safer places for us to visit. We are invited to walk around in the rooms of Betsy's words, notice what is on the walls, the coffee table, in the oven. We may take a seat and ponder what the words hold for us.

Thank you, Betsy, for keeping your hands off your words, offering us sanctuary.

Betsy's voice does more. Her voice conjures to awareness the oft forgotten and unattended voices we carry around---the sound, color, grain of memory, imagination, joy, sorrow, peace, regret and reconciliation. We are inspired, healed, encouraged.

As I reflect on Betsy's words just now, I am carried back south to my "dirt," as my sister says. The smell of cigar around Betsy's dad and a first flight to LaGrange, Georgia to participate in a spelling bee place me in the stands of the Albany, Georgia High School football stadium.

I smell Mr. Gerst's cigar two seats away, my dad between us. The LaGrange Grangers on the far side of the field, the Albany Indians on the near side. All rise and cheer as the Indian marching band comes down the hill and onto the field playing *Dixie*, the letter girls leading the way waving the Confederate flag.

Now I remember Mr. Gerst's jubilant shout from the sidewalk outside his furniture store, next to my dad's clothing store. He's just heard of President Kennedy's death: "They finally got that communist son-of-a-bitch."

Remembered dirt arouses more mindful engagement with what is. The present takes on a textured hue.

Albany High School then, Ferguson, Missouri now. Charlotte Public Library then, North Charleston now. Decatur, Georgia High School then, Charleston's Mother Emmanuel Church now. Betsy's sheltering dad and mom. My violent dad and justifiably melancholic mom. My day gains weight and density, ascends to lament. I hear Flannery O'Connor's voice, "All that rises must converge." Betsy and Flannery. What a morning!

Betsy takes us places. Places we need to go. Jim Crow has gone underground. He's present and insidious. Stealth. Betsy helps us name him.

Betsy is wise. *Momma's stories opened us up to our own stories.* Another Look evokes. Betsy's book is invocation, a read that is a hearing-together-in community, an experience, as Betsy says, *that can only be described as grace.*

I am delighted that you, the reader, are joining us. I imagine and anticipate that a handful of the more dormant voices we carry around will become audible again as if for the first time, will give rise to new voices and articulation for the good.

Bill Blaine-Wallace
Farmington, Maine
Early Fall, 2015

Introduction

In the 1940's when I was a child there was a popular song called *Long Ago and Far Away* by Jerome Kern and Ira Gershwin. Rita Hayworth sang it to Gene Kelly in the movie *Cover Girl*. I know this song because it was often on the radio, and I learned all the words. When I began gathering the stories in this collection, the song kept running in my head. And while many of the events I write about happened a long time ago, they remain vivid, shaping in part the person I have become. I am the keeper of the old stories as well as their grown up narrator.

What follows is a brief family history that may help to put the stories into context. As I look again at the history and tell the stories, I sometimes find my lens shifting, depending on the place and time from which I see them.

My parents named me Elizabeth Holland in honor of my father's sister and my mother's brother. I was the youngest of three children. My brother Jerry was two years older than me, and my sister Meg was a huge six years older. She seemed almost like a grownup. We lived in a little house on the campus of Queens College in Charlotte, North Carolina, where my father was Dean. The house had once been painted white, but in my memory it is grayish with a small, roofed front porch facing the street.

The most important part of the house was the big back porch with steep wooden stairs that ran up to the kitchen door. That door opened and closed all day long as students knocked and came right on in without waiting. They knew they were always welcome and Momma was sure to have a pot of warm coffee and a smile ready to greet them. Daddy used to say that more counseling went on in the kitchen than ever happened in his office.

As children we led a charmed life with plenty of room to run where we liked. We grew up with a strong ethic of good behavior, kindness and curiosity. Most of all there was a lot of laughter and music. Daddy played the piano by ear and taught us western songs, show tunes, old time love songs, hymns, and even arias from opera. Late afternoon before supper we'd almost always find Daddy at the piano. We were welcome to join in, and my sister Meg, who had a sweet, big soprano voice, usually did. I easily learned all the words, but uncertain of my voice, I was often reluctant to join in the singing.

Momma's contribution was stories. She read aloud to us, always at bedtime, and often during the day if the time felt right. Robinson Crusoe and Captain Hook remain vivid in my memory. She once held our attention for over a week reading a condensed tale of Shakespeare's *Julius Caesar*. When she asked us what we thought of it, my brother Jerry thought for a few minutes and said, "Well, you can't always trust the people you think are your friends." He went on to describe being betrayed by his former friend Kenny. I remember feeling relieved when he told us about this. I had never liked Kenny, and now I knew why. Momma's stories opened us up to our own stories, and we got to know each other better that way.

I loved all the reading aloud from books, but what I loved most was Momma's telling the old Southern stories aloud in dialect. We came to know Bre'er Rabbit well, and Eeyore the old gray donkey felt like our buddy, especially when one of us was sad. Jerry and I sometimes took the parts of the characters and acted out our own stories.

Life changed abruptly the year I turned twelve. We moved to Decatur, Georgia, a small town on the edge of Atlanta. It was a shock. I learned more about life's unfairness, especially when it came to race. I had spent my childhood living in a college community that had been protected in many ways. We were now in a house that looked like every other small ranch house in this post World War II neighborhood. The bleached blonde woman next door yelled at her "pesky chilren" all day long. The sound hurt my ears and my heart. We didn't yell in our house.

Daddy had taken a position as Director of the college accreditation association for the Southern states. His mandate was to lead the predominantly black colleges to the same standards required of white colleges. He traveled a lot, and I went with him some of the time that summer. No one knew what else to do with me. I was too young to be left alone all day in a strange town, and too old to need a baby sitter. Momma, who had been home all of my life, was updating her credentials for a teaching job in a private school across town. Meg worked as a hospital aide and then went off to college. Jerry worked in a tire factory all summer and came home exhausted and covered in black tarry stuff. He didn't play with me any more. My cozy little world was gone. That summer I pulled out my hair, strand by golden strand. No one noticed for a long time.

But children are resilient, and by October, I'd recovered, found a new way to wear my hair, and settled in. Meg went off to Duke, and for the first time in my life, I had a bedroom all to myself. Jerry was the very popular defensive back on the high school football team, and all of the girls were nice to me because of him. I was even elected secretary of my class.

When Daddy's tenure was successfully completed, we moved again - this time to Coral Gables, Florida, where Daddy was Vice President of the University of Miami. Momma left teaching and was at home again. I loved the new town, new school, and new friends. Jerry went off to college at Auburn, and I was the only child at home. Heaven!

I went to college at Tulane and studied English literature. I did well, though I never loved college as my siblings had. But I did get to spend an entire year in England at a red brick university only thirty miles from London. I studied Shakespeare and Yeats and took the train to the London theaters, usually with a friend. Since we often missed the return curfew in the dorm, I left a window open for us to climb in. This was common practice, and no one blew the whistle on us as long as we were discreet. I fell in love with a graduate student who followed me back home. For a short time it was thrilling, but he somehow looked very different on this side of the ocean. Soon after his arrival, he moved across the country.

I met Frank, the forever love of my life when I was twenty-two. I had a graduate fellowship that I could take anywhere in the United States, and I chose the University of Pennsylvania because the English department was strong. That lucky choice was to mark my whole life. Frank was finishing medical school there and was headed for internship in New York. We married when he began residency at the end of a grueling internship. Even as a resident, he worked long hours every day, and was on call every other night and every other weekend. I got a job teaching English literature at Adelphi University on Long Island. I loved teaching and had the good fortune to commute against traffic. We lived in the city at a house staff residence attached to the hospital by a paging system, telephones, and a tunnel that ran under York Avenue. We had little money and less time. We were young, and we loved every busy, overpriced minute of life in New York.

The Vietnam War was in full swing when Frank's medical training ended, and the draft was looming. All young physicians were obligated to military service. There was a process called the Berry Plan, which allowed young doctors to complete their internship and residency trainings before embarking on two years in the military. The simple reasoning was that the service got the benefit of their advanced training, and the young physicians could practice their skills and return to civilian society. The possibility that they might return damaged, or not at all was seldom mentioned. Neither of us supported the war in principle, but did not even entertain the possibility of dissent by leaving the country. Military service was, after all, the law of the land.

Frank trained as a hematologist and was sent to Fort Knox, Kentucky. It was a major armored tank center but it also had a significant blood-banking component. The base was a shipping out point for Vietnam and was filled to capacity, with healthy young men departing, and damaged ones returning to be treated at Ireland Army Hospital. As there was no available housing on the base, we rented a farmhouse about thirteen miles down the Dixie Highway. We had one neighbor family who did not like city folks or military ones. We qualified on both counts and led a pretty solitary life. Frank did receive orders for Vietnam, but they were mercifully cancelled a few weeks before he was to ship out. His commanding colonel watched with sadness as the promotion that had dangled before him if his platoon went to Vietnam vanished before his eyes. We were relieved to keep our family together and to spend our last months of army life in this country. Despite its limits, Fort Knox topped Saigon by a long way. Our rented and remote farmhouse was not the garden spot of the world, but it sure beat an Asian war zone. We now had two very young sons, George and Ted.

From Kentucky we returned to New York for a year before moving on to Boston, where our family grew to three sons, the last one named Andrew. We also acquired an assortment of dogs. We bought a house in a good school district, thinking we'd be here just a few years before moving on. Forty-five years later we are still in the same house. Frank is still at the Harvard Medical School. He has enjoyed a hugely fulfilling and successful career as research scientist, physician, and professor. The boys have grown up and moved away with their own families. I taught part time and became a long distance runner in those early years, finally completing a full marathon the year I turned forty. As the children became more independent, my life expanded wonderfully in a way that I could not have predicted. The hospice movement was beginning in this country, and we lived by chance near a home care hospice that was just opening. It had been designated a demonstration project, first by Blue Cross and soon after by Medicare. I trained to be a volunteer there, working in the office as well as assisting patients and family members in whatever non-medical tasks needed to be done. I came to know many very special people. I learned a lot about human frailty and strength and about what I can only describe as grace. It was a deep privilege. I began to take courses at the local community college and became a licensed social worker. I moved on to work in two more hospices as they developed over the next fifteen years. During that time, I also led a discussion group for Harvard students, staff and faculty who were affected by serious illness or loss. All of this fit together, feeling like what I was meant to do. Many years later I remain honored and blessed by this work experience. I retired soon after our five grandsons began their entry to the world, so that I might have the privilege and the joy of knowing them as they grew up.

I offer these stories as insights into a time that is past, the enduring essence of which remains strong. The writing falls into three areas: 1) stories of growing up in the Jim Crow South, 2) stories of life in the South later, and 3) essays on several topics that have captured my imagination and aroused my concerns in recent years.

I. The Jim Crow South

First Day of School

Library Lessons

Dark Water

Back Home

These four stories begin when I was six and extend well into adulthood, all of them marked by Jim Crow, a set of formal and informal laws enacted after what Southerners called *The War Between the States* or *The War of Northern Aggression*. History books describe it as *The Civil War*. Jim Crow laws were enacted and enforced by a depleted South to perpetuate the perceived need to keep Negroes "in their place." That meant segregating blacks from whites in almost

every way possible, except as servants. There was a well-known song about the character Jim Crow, a dim witted black slave, usually played by a white man in black face. Jim Crow was happy-go-lucky, slow of mind, and lazy. The song was called "Jump Jim Crow." I thought it was a catchy song until the day my parents heard me singing it and gave me a serious spanking. This marked the beginning of my long confusion about race, since I knew that my thoughtful, liberal parents viewed spanking as a last resort for incorrigible behavior. They worked to move the culture forward while maintaining some sense of safety within the rigid white social structure. The times were unclear even to adults, and totally baffling to a child.

I noticed that most of the people who worked in our neighborhood were colored women who came on a bus. They always carried umbrellas to shield them from both sun and rain, and they all left by the same bus around 3:00 every afternoon. But we had friends, Marshalljunior and Louise, who were also colored. They lived near us in a little cottage on the campus. Their father, Big Marshall worked at the college. He was in charge of buildings and grounds and he could fix almost anything, even my old blue hand-me-down bike. Jerry and

I played with Marshalljunior and Louise almost every day in the summer and the four of us often ate lunch together. Louise and I made a telephone with paper cups and string that ran from their cottage to our house. All of my other friends were white. I noticed, but I didn't know that it mattered—not until I was older.

Sometimes when it was pouring rain or scorching hot, Momma would drive our day helper Herculine home in the car so she wouldn't have to wait for the bus or walk home from the last stop. I liked the ride. Often we would have to wait at the railroad tracks while a long, long train passed. I counted the cars as high as I could count. One day Herculine laughed and said, "I reckon some folks has to wait to get into Colored Town, and some folks is never able to get out of there." When I asked if there was a White Town, she said that was just most other places and didn't have a name. I thought living in Colored Town must be pretty special.

I never spent time in Herc's house, but I did sometimes get to go with her to church on Sundays. The service went on for hours – much longer than the services in our church. There was lots of singing, and the sermon was long and loud. The colored folks seemed to have more fun at church than we did in our quiet Presbyterian worship. One time when I was there, everyone was singing, and a woman who was wearing a great big straw hat with flowers began to shout and sway. Then she fell down in the aisle. An usher went to help her, and the preacher shouted, "Leave her lay, brother. Leave her lay where Jesus flang her." I was hugely relieved when she got to her feet a few minutes later.

It is my intent and hope that these stories may catch the flavor of a particular time in the South, and the experience through which one child tried to make sense of life. *The First Day of School*, describes my excitement over finally being sufficiently grown up to join my brother and our friends at school and some of the disillusionment that follows. In *Library Lessons*, my brother Jerry learns more about privilege and exclusion as he has a chance to help Momma do what she can for the movement toward racial change. In *Dark Water*, Jerry and I find ourselves in a situation in which our colored friend has privilege that we do not and strength we did not know. *Back Home* takes place 30 years later and walks through my family's history. It continues to surprise me with its ongoing revelations.

II. Stories, Mostly Southern, Past and Thereafter

Lost and found

Lost as a Rabbit

Momma's Dream

Worth Troubling Over

The Picture Show

The Gas Can

Look Again

These stories cast a broader net. They are family stories with characters from my grandmother's generation on down to the generation of my children and theirs. They promise, as the last one declares, that we will look again at the past.

The first story, *Lost and Found*, is set in Kentucky where we lived for two years during the Viet Nam War. It moves through present and past and brings up questions about the nature of body and soul. There was considerable superstition about restless souls in Southern culture. Stories of "hants" coming back were whispered in both colored and white evangelical churches and sometimes even told outright from the pulpit.

We lived in a country farmhouse not unlike the one described in this story. We did indeed have clay pipes and a plumber, and a long dirt road where little felt solid or real. I wrote this story soon after we left Kentucky in 1968. Years later I ran into a splendid drawing by Bryan Andras called *The Plumber* that influenced this version of the story. I have also been amused by the Sesame Street enacting of the parrot, which falls down dead after getting no reply to his loud and lengthy cries of "It's the plumber. I came to fix the sink."

Momma (My mother, Aura Holton Godard, 1903-1988) appears in the next three stories, each of which happened in real, though widespread, time. *Lost as a Rabbit* describes her poignant recalling of a phrase she had used casually as a metaphor when she was young to describe her now profound terror of loss in old age. In *Momma's Dream* she experiences a recurring and frightening dream, only to discover that it finds a different ending and emotional resolution. The phrase *Worth Troubling Over* starts as part of a kitchen conversation that suddenly takes on a whole new meaning and reverberates through our family history.

The last three stories in this section remain in the family, moving forward to my generation and that of my children. *The Picture Show* describes an experience I had as a not-quite teenager in Decatur, Georgia. Wanting to be taken as much older than my eleven years, I found myself in an uncomfortable and frightening situation and had to figure my way out of it. *The Gas Can* returns to the issue of race, still unresolved in the next generation. My oldest son George remained in the South when he finished his service in the Navy, and worked his way through community college and university. He has shown up for some rough jobs along the way, and his experience with race has been irregular at best. This story has an improbable hero.

The title for this collection, *Another Look*, takes its name from the last story in this section. I have come to realize that many of life's experiences are part of a chain that forms our character and shapes the person we become. As *I Look Again* at my own life from youth to the present, and revisit lives that are woven into mine, I make new discoveries. In this story I am recalling one of the principles my father taught us, beginning when we were very young: "If someone steals something from you, he probably needs it more than you did. Bear him no ill will and consider your own blessings."

I never argued this matter with my father. I had learned that sometimes keeping my mouth shut was the better part of wisdom. But I didn't believe him. I'd been taught the Ten Commandments in Sunday school, and "Thou shalt not steal" made a lot of simple sense to my young mind. As I recount this story to Rebecca, a much loved daughter in law, I begin to discern the subtle truth of Daddy's teaching.

III. Essays

Suddenly I'm History

How I See It

The Walk Back

The Well

The last part of this book contains four essays that touch on the passage of time. Written in my own later years, they reflect on the present and the past.

Suddenly, I'm History begins as my grown children laugh gently at photos of their Momma in the fifties. I revisit my own perceptions of what was happening at that time and how I made sense of life.

In *How I See It*, the house where we currently live feels compelled to write its own history, focusing on the 45 years we lived within its walls. We have grown together as both the family and the house expanded over time. When we moved into the house, it was somewhat dark and very tidy. There were heavy green drapes with white scrim panels filling the space between the drapes. The view from inside was always dim, and it was totally impossible to see inside the house from the outside. Our predecessors liked privacy. As our family grew and settled, the house grew also. It opened up to the neighborhood, the natural world around us, and the activity of our own lives. Doors and windows were often left open. We rarely locked the front door unless we were out of town. The house has experienced floods, ice dams, and frogs croaking from the pond.

The Walk Back moves from the house to the area surrounding it. The nearby woods and river tell their own story, and ours. This walk back in time and experience is set on a small peninsula of the Charles River. There are ninety homes adjoining a large field that borders the water. For many years the field was home to the Norumbega Amusement Park with its rides and gardens and music. Some of the greatest bands of the 1930's and 40's played here. Benny Goodman and Dinah Shore made frequent appearances, as did Frankie Lane and the Dorsey Brothers. Now it is a quiet place, designated as open space, with tall grass and dogs and some fine trees to climb. I walk here often, touched by sun and snow, and reveling in the quiet. There is a sense of history, enhanced by remnants of the past; footings of a great Ferris wheel lie amid overgrown paths that once ran through orderly gardens.

The Well moves much further back in time, to the days when we fetched water for drinking. It considers both what we have gained with progress and what we have lost. And it offers a recommendation for shaping the future, if there is to be one.

It is a great privilege to have the opportunity to remember the fullness of the past, to grow from history, and to share its richness with others. I am grateful indeed to remember and to see these memories in a broader light as I take *Another Look*.

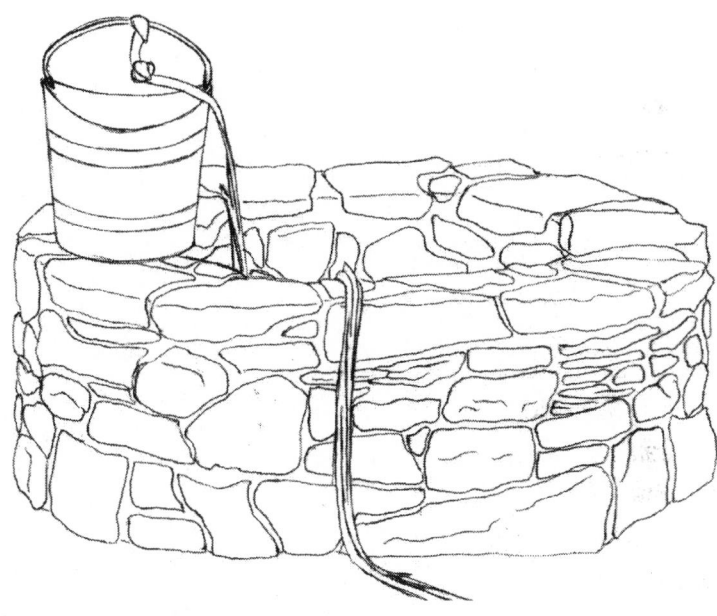

I. The Jim Crow South

FIRST DAY OF SCHOOL

When I was six, going on seven, I knew some things for sure. My whole name was Elizabeth Holland, but everyone called me Betsy. I knew my address, just in case I ever got lost. My phone number was 2-1562. I had a Momma and a Daddy and a brother named Jerry, who was eight going on nine, and a sister named Meg, who was twelve. We lived on the college campus where our Daddy worked. We had a dog named Nicky, and she came from the dog pound. Her first owners had called her Niggy because she was black and brown. Momma said that wasn't nice – something about colored people – and so we changed her name to Nicky. Momma said it sounded kind of the same, so it wouldn't confuse the dog.

That was my family, not counting the aunts and uncles and cousins. I was the youngest, even counting the dog and the cousins. I was allowed to play anywhere on our side of the street between the back porch steps and the reflecting pool in the campus courtyard, just as long as I could hear Momma if she called. But I could never cross the street alone or go into the main campus grounds without a grown up. Those were the things I knew for sure.

I played alone a lot, but I was also lucky to have friends on my side of the street. I can't remember a time when I didn't know Marshalljunior and Louise. They were my best friends. Louise was a year older than me, and Marshalljunior was just a little bit older than Jerry. Sometimes I got to play with Lillian and Grant too. But they lived across the street, so I only saw them when a grown up crossed me and knew where I was.

Lillian and Grant were older than me. Everyone was older than me. I was a little afraid of Lillian. She had red ringlets and bright blue eyes and a bad temper. Once when she got tired of playing with me, she chased me with a pitchfork. Another time she wanted to go off with Jerry and play some private game called "you show me." She wouldn't let me come because I was only six, and she said I was a baby.

Grant was Jerry's special friend. He was almost always nice to me. He let me play baseball with the boys even when Jerry wouldn't, and he let me walk to first base when he was pitching. He never let me be "IT" for long in games of Kick the Can either. He'd make a noise so I could find him, and then he'd usually trip over something and fall, so I could beat him to home base. I was pretty sure he did it on purpose, but I never said so because I was afraid he might stop. He and Jerry sometimes got into trouble. One time when our street was being repaved, they rolled in the new tar so they could turn black. Grant said he wanted to drive a garbage truck when he grew up, and everyone knew you had to be colored to do that. I remember Momma got really mad at them, and it took a long time to scrub them clean.

Marhshalljunior and Louise and I played almost every day. We made great piles of leaves to hide in. Twice a year we were allowed to stay up late and watch huge leaf bonfires on the college athletic field and then sleep over at each other's houses. Sometimes we went creek hopping in the woods beyond the range of Momma's voice and played at being Tarzan and Jane and the apes. One summer we made up a complicated game called Moses and the Bull Rushes.

Marshalljunior was tall and skinny. He could move through the woods so quietly that not even a stick cracked. He was always Tonto when we played Cowboys and Indians. Jerry was the Lone Ranger, and Louise and I had to be squaws. At the end of the summer, Marshalljunior and Jerry could break a piece of green Coke bottle glass with their bare heels. Louise and I tried to get tough enough to do that. She did pretty well, but all I got was a string of bloody heels. Momma would shake her head and say, "Now Missy, I can see how your knees get all skinned up cause you fall down on your skates, but I can't make out for the life of me what happens to your feet. Your heels are all scabby. Do they hurt?"

I shook my head and blinked. I didn't want to lie, and I couldn't tell the truth. Girls weren't allowed to go barefoot so I always went outside with my shoes on and then hid them in the creek bank. Jerry teased me about not having "summer feet," but he never told on me. He knew Momma would get really mad if she knew.

Jerry and Meg, Lillian and Grant and Marshalljunior and Louise all went to school. Myers Park Grammar School was less than a mile from the campus. I'd wanted to go there for as long as I could remember. And finally this was the year I would start first grade. I almost got to go last year, but my birthday was too late. It was only a week after the cut off date, and Momma tried to get the superintendent to bend the rules so I could start. But he wouldn't budge. "Now Missy," Momma said. "There are some rules that just don't bend, and I reckon that's one of them." So they sent me to a special program at the college and they called it school. But it wasn't real school at all. They didn't read or spell or add. They mostly played and sang songs. I could already read and spell and add a little bit, and I hated this fake school. The only good parts were recess and snack. But soon I would go to real school, and next year when I turned seven, I would cross the street alone if I promised to look both ways first.

I got up early that first morning. I remember the smell of bacon and coffee that Daddy made every morning. I brushed my hair a hundred times. I could already count way past a hundred. I put on the blue-checkered dress that Momma had set out the night before and went to Momma to have my hair braided. I squeezed my eyes tight shut before Momma started, because the way she braided, my eyes would be pulled out of shape all day if I didn't close them first. Momma finished the long braids off with rubber bands and tied blue ribbons on them. I could tie and even double tie my own oxfords, but the hair ribbons were too slippery. I turned all the way around for Momma's inspection.

She smiled, "You look just fine, Missy. Now off you go. Daddy will walk you to school today, and tomorrow you can walk with the other children." I opened my mouth to protest because I'd been looking forward to going off with the big kids today. But I could tell from Momma's face that this was another one of those rules that wasn't going to bend. I reached up for Daddy's hand and we marched off. I had to walk very fast, because Daddy had such big long legs. I started to skip, so it would look like I was having fun instead of running to keep up.

We got to school, and Daddy walked me all the way to the first grade classroom. He introduced me to my teacher, Miss Wilcox. She was tall and gray haired and smelled like roses. The room smelled like pencils and green disinfectant and chalk. The desks were all screwed to the floor, and I got my very own. I looked around. I knew about half the kids in the class from church or because their parents worked at the college. I settled into my seat. A big kid at last! I could hardly wait for recess when I could find Louise on the playground.

Recess came at ten o'clock. I'd been watching the big round clock in front of the room because Meg said that was recess time. I could tell time perfectly, even to the minute. We lined up, and Miss Wilcox said that we could play in the first area of the playground, and half of grades one to three would be out this period. I raced to the jungle gym as soon as the line broke. Grant was already there, grinning from the top square. I climbed up to the middle and looked around. I didn't want to climb too high because I had on a dress that day instead of summer shorts. I was afraid my skirt would blow up. Once when Betty Jo had worn a blowy skirt to the church picnic, the boys made a ring around her and chanted, "I see London, I see France. I see Betty Jo's underpants" until Betty Jo cried. I'd been careful about dresses ever since. Didn't wear them except to church unless Momma made me. Today was one of those days.

The playground was huge. I looked around for Louise. I saw Lillian on the swings, her red ringlets bouncing with each pump up and back. Jerry ran by with a football, but he didn't seem to notice me. I didn't see Louise anywhere, and then the bell rang and we had to go in.

The time till lunch went fast. Miss Wilcox passed out spelling books and said there would be a spelling bee every Friday, and the best speller in each class would get to go to the state spelling bee in November. I looked ahead to the last page in the book, and I knew every single word on the list. Meg had gone to the state bee one year, and I wanted to go and maybe even win. I'd get her to practice with me.

When the lunch bell rang, Miss Wilcox walked us down to the lunchroom. She said we'd eat with the other half of grades one to three and then have about fifteen minutes on the playground. The lunchroom was crowded and noisy. I looked around for

Marshalljunior and Louise. I wondered what they'd brought for lunch. I had a meat loaf sandwich with ketchup, and the ketchup had soaked through the bread. I ate most of it fast and went outside.

It was baking hot. The heat came up from the concrete and down from the sky and there was no breeze at all. It was hard to see in the glare. I squinted my eyes tight and walked around, trying to look like I was going somewhere, but really looking for Louise. Lillian was playing jump rope way over under the magnolia tree, and Meg was out watching because she was in the sixth grade and got to be a playground monitor. I almost walked over to them, but I wasn't sure Lillian would be nice to me. I wasn't very good at jump rope yet. She might make fun of me. So I walked the other way. I couldn't find Louise or Marshalljunior anywhere. Finally the bell rang. It was cooler inside and the first big day was almost over.

When we were back in our desks, Miss Wilcox gave out reading books and divided us up into groups with bird names. I was a bluebird. The book was about Dick and Jane and Spot. It was kind of dumb but I liked that I knew all the words. Then we drew for a while – balloons on a stick and triangle trees. I wasn't very good at drawing. I hoped it wouldn't matter too much.

When the bell rang at 2:30, Meg was already waiting for me. She asked me all about my day: the teacher, the playground, the spelling bee, and who sat in front of me and behind. We were almost home. I stopped and said, "Meg, I saw Grant on the jungle gym and Susan and Betty Jo from church, and Lillian and Jerry. But I didn't see Marshalljunior or Louise. Not at recess or lunch. Can we stop at their house for just a minute on our way home?"

Meg looked at me all funny and didn't answer. Then she shook her head and said, "No, I don't think so. It's really hot, and besides I have to go to the bathroom. C'mon I'll race you to the kitchen." She took off. I ran after her. But I couldn't keep up, and I felt all hot and little again. I stumbled on the back porch stairs. But I didn't cry. The kitchen was cool, and Momma was there, and there was cold lemonade in the pink bubbly pitcher and the smell of freshly ironed sheets.

"Well, well, well, it's my big girls home from school," said Momma. "Come on in and tell me all about it."

I took a big gulp of lemonade and then said, "Oh Momma, it was fun, and I can spell better than anybody, and I have my own desk right behind Betty Jo, and we got to play outside two times. But Momma, I couldn't find Marshalljunior or Louise anywhere. They weren't at recess so I thought they'd be at lunch. But I looked and looked, and they weren't there either. Can I call them to come over now? Please Momma, please can I?"

The kitchen was suddenly very still. Meg squirmed in her chair and looked at the floor. "Momma," she said quietly, "we never told her. We must've forgot. She doesn't know."

I glared at Meg. "What don't I know? I'm not a baby. You better tell me."

Momma said softly, "Why, it never occurred to me she didn't know." She looked back at Meg, but Meg had turned her back and was pouring sugar in the lemonade. Momma took a deep breath and looked right at me. "Colored children can't go to school with white children, Baby. Marshalljunior and Louise won't ever go to school with you."

I began to cry. Meg tried to comfort me. "Don't cry, Baby, please don't cry. They go to another school someplace else. They don't mind. They have other friends, and you will too. You don't need them any more. It's okay. You'll see. It's all okay."

I stared at them, stunned. Then I ran. I hid in my closet and scrunched up as small as I could. I was never coming out. Not ever.

I was six years old and there were some things I knew for sure. My name was Betsy. I had a Momma and a Daddy and a brother and a sister. And a dog we called Nicky. I couldn't cross the street yet – not till I was seven.

Now I knew a new thing. Momma and Meg said it was for sure. My best friends would never go to school with me. They were the wrong color, and so they weren't allowed, Momma said. Not ever.

I had thought that going to school would open up my world. Instead, it began to close it down. Meg was wrong. It was not okay.

Library Lessons

Jerry was eight and a half years old. He was in the third grade at school, and he liked it now. But he'd got off to a bumpy start learning to read in the first grade. Momma said later that she thought it was just that crazy new teaching method. Jerry reported that Miss Thompson would hold up a picture with a word under it, and the children were all supposed to look at it and remember what the word was and how to spell it. Like "*wagon*." Some kids got it right away, but he wasn't one of them. After the first few weeks, Miss Thompson called Momma in for a conference and told her that Jerry just wasn't very bright. Certainly not as bright as his big sister, Meg. He was well behaved and seemed to pay attention, but was not retaining the words. They were using a highly recommended new way of teaching called *Look and Learn*. She thought he would need special classes.

Momma listened and kept her thoughts to herself, saying only, "Well, let's give it a little time, maybe a month or so, and then we'll see." She was pretty sure that by sounding out words that interested him, Jerry would get hold of reading. He was plenty smart. So she and

Daddy joined forces. Using the newspaper, they helped him sound out whatever caught his interest. They started with the "funnies" in the Sunday paper. He liked the strips of *Gasoline Alley* and *Elmer Fudd* and *Blondie and Dagwood*. Pretty soon he was reading all the comic pages. I was two and a half years younger, and he would read them to me. *Blondie and Dagwood* was my favorite. He liked baseball too, and knew a lot about it. He and Daddy regularly listened on the radio to the games of the Charlotte Hornets. So Daddy showed him how to read the box scores in the newspaper for all the teams in the division. His hero was Lefty Brewer, who pitched winning seasons until 1943 when he went away to join the army and never came back. By the end of the month, Miss Thompson had called Momma to report that Jerry was doing fine, and she guessed he had just been a slow starter.

There was no stopping him after that. Now there was nothing he couldn't read. Not just pictures and sports either. He read about how things worked, and how far away the sun was, and what was in the ocean. He could see pictures in the stars at night. And bears and warriors. He began to show me how the letters sounded. He'd chant, "A is for apple; B is for bike and also for Betsy, which is your name!"

We lived on a college campus where our Daddy was a dean. After school, Jerry played mostly with our friend Marshall. He was ten years old and lived on the campus too. We called him Marshalljunior. His Daddy, Big Marshall, was head of maintenance. He could fix almost everything, and often would let Jerry and Marshalljunior go with him when he had to go way down to the basement under a class building or a dormitory to fix leaking pipes or check the heating. He could even make the electricity come back after a thunderstorm. Sometimes the boys sneaked off underground by themselves. One time I followed them down there under the dining hall. They had flashlights, but I didn't take one because I was afraid they'd see me. I was scared of the dark, but even more scared they'd find me. So I had to stay close, but not too close. I could hear them talking.

"They's spies down here," Marshalljunior said.

"Shh," said Jerry. "They'll hear us."

"I got my bowie knife," whispered Marshalljunior as they turned a corner and the pipes got lower. I could see Jerry hunch over. I could barely stand. They were both taller than me, so I guessed Marshalljunior must be crawling. I brushed into a spider web. I wanted to turn back, but I was afraid I'd be lost in the maze of pipes. I tripped, and Jerry heard me.

"Hey, man," he called to Marshalljunior. He sounded scared. "Something else is down here with us."

"Probably rats," said Marshalljunior. "Just keep moving."

That was too much. My fear of rats was greater than my fear of being caught, so I called out and they found me. Jerry was really mad that I had sneaked along, but Marshalljunior said it was okay, just not to do it ever again. He managed to crawl in front of me and lead the way out.

When we saw the light at the end, we all swore not to tell where we'd been. I never went down there again, but they always told me when they were going, just in case something went wrong. I made them promise to be back in an hour, or I'd tell on them. Momma never found out. She'd have spanked Jerry good if she had known.

Saturdays were special for both of us. Jerry went to the library with Momma while I had a playtime with Daddy. We usually went over to the campus. It was a fun walk through the woods, down the curly walk, past the statue of Diana in the goldfish pond and into the Burwell Building where Daddy had his office. I had memorized the words carved into sidewalk at the end of the curly walk.

> "*Though this path leads just to college,*
> *Still it bears a wealth of knowledge.*

She who walks this simple way
Will walk a greater path someday."

Sometimes one of Daddy's students would come to read or play with me, and that was fun. But mostly I looked forward to the time when I would be old enough to go to the library on Saturdays with Momma and Jerry. I could already read some. Momma said when I turned seven, they'd take me along.

Jerry loved the trip to the library. It was a big brick building with arched windows. There were stairs going up both sides to a wide double doorway. It was called the Carnegie Library because Andrew Carnegie gave the money to build it. Jerry had his own library card and was allowed to get seven new books each week, as long as he brought the other ones back. He could wander by himself through the shelves and choose whatever he wanted to read. The librarian said that Momma should stay with him and "direct his choices," but Momma told her that he knew what he wanted to read better than she did, and besides she had her own books to choose. A lot of them. She and Jerry agreed on a time to meet at the check out desk. He was careful to see that Momma got there before he did. The first few times he got there first and had to defend his choices to the librarian. She thought the book on stars was way too difficult, and she was sure he'd never get through the myths about the Greek gods. *"How about Bible Stories for Children?"* she asked. But Momma came up and looked at his books and assured her that he could handle them all. Meanwhile she had her own cart, filled with all of the books her *Friend of the Library* card allowed. The librarian just sighed and checked them both out.

Jerry sometimes wondered why Momma got all those books, but just figured grown ups could do that. He knew he'd get more if he could.

One day as they were headed to the library, Jerry could tell Momma had something on her mind. And sure enough, while they were driving, she said, "Now Jerrison, there's something I need to tell you. Should have done it sooner." She paused. "Maybe you know; maybe you figured it out." They were almost at the library, and she waited till she had parked to continue. Jerry just sat there. Quiet. She took a deep breath and went on, "Well, you and I can just walk right up those stairs and inside whenever we want to. We can borrow and return books, seven for children, and a cartload for me." Jerry waited.

She took a deep breath and continued. "But Negroes can't go in there. Not ever. Your friend Marshalljunior would not be allowed in here. Not even if he came with you and me." Jerry opened his mouth, but no sound came out. He'd known for a long time that Marshalljunior went to a different school because he was colored. He'd missed him at first, but got used to playing with him at home, just as they had always done. It wasn't like he didn't have a school of his own, after all. But to be denied the library? That was unthinkable. He might as well be kept out of Heaven! Maybe he was! God probably knew he was colored.

Jerry was quiet. Taking it in. "But Momma, that's just wrong!"

"I know," she said, " and someday it will change, but meantime we've got things to do. Today when we get our books, I'd like you to help me get them to folks who can't come here. I've been doing it for a while, and I could use a hand. Come along now, and remember to keep your own books separate to go home. Maybe put them under the seat."

I began to notice that they were gone longer on Saturdays than they used to be. Daddy and I would get home before they did. I asked what took them so long, and Momma said they just had a few extra things to do. I liked my Saturdays with Daddy okay, but I looked forward to my birthday, so I could go to the library too.

The day came. We started off early that first Saturday. When the library opened at 10:00, we were waiting at the door. Momma took us both up to the desk and explained that Jerry and I would be coming to choose our books together on Saturdays now and would meet her at a specified time to check out. Momma was very polite, but I could tell that the librarian – her name was Miss Allen – didn't like the plan. Jerry had figured out a way to maximize our reading. We could each get seven books, making a total of fourteen. So he proposed that we pick four books each, and then choose six that we both liked. That way each of us would have ten books a week. It sounded fine to me, though I hoped Jerry wouldn't bulldoze me. Momma turned left toward the adult books, and we went downstairs to the children/young adult section. Jerry and I chose our books easily and were pleased with ourselves. We both liked the dog books by Alfred Terhune and the Freddy series by Walter Brooks. Tarzan was a winner too.

In half an hour, we met Momma back at the desk. She had her pushcart filled. I knew I'd never seen her bring that many books home. There must have been dozens. I opened my mouth to ask why she had so many. Then I looked up at Miss Allen's pinched face and decided not to ask anything. We just checked out and went to the car.

Instead of heading home, Momma drove through downtown Charlotte and then across the train tracks toward the part of town that people called Colored Town. I didn't think that was its real name, but I recognized it right away because we had driven by Daddy Grace's house down by Sugar Creek a few times. It was huge. A mansion set way back on the green lawn, with two lion statues out front. There was a tall wrought iron fence around the house, and just beyond it, outside the fence, was a small white church. Daddy Grace was the big time preacher for the colored community. I'd seen him around town, driving a fancy black car and wearing a hat and a three-piece suit.

On this trip Momma drove around the big house and parked just beyond the fence, right next to the church. There was no sign of Daddy Grace. But there were lots of colored folks standing around outside -- children and grown ups. They'd set up four card tables, with room to walk all around each one. The men came to help Momma unload the books and put them on the tables. Jerry told me to put my books next to his under the back seat of the car so they wouldn't get picked up by mistake, and we got out to help. He put a big card that said "RETURNS" on one table. Momma said we should stand there and keep the books from falling off. When they piled up, we could put them in the now empty cart. People began to look through the new books and help themselves. One by one, they chose a book, and then came to the table where Momma stood with her notebook. She'd write down the name of the book and ask the person's name. Then she'd ask if they'd brought back a book to the Returns table. Mostly they said, "Yes, thank you," and then just walked away. I knew that all those books were signed out in Momma's name!

"Momma, they can't just take your books," I whispered to her.

But she just smiled and said to each person, "Bring that book back next Saturday please. I'll have more, but I have to return these to get them." I just looked at her. I kept my mouth shut, but I was kind of scared. What if they didn't bring the books back? Would Momma get in trouble? Would we be still be able to get our books?

On the way home, she explained to me what Jerry already knew. He had been helping her with the books for over a year now. She told me that Negroes were not allowed in our library because of something called Jim Crow laws. The law said that the state had to provide a separate library for Negroes. But the one that had been "provided" was a tiny shack out near the river with only a few books and no staff. And even that poor place was rarely open. So Daddy and Momma had made a plan. Until I turned seven, Daddy would take care of me on Saturdays while she and Jerry took books to Colored Town. They had done it for a long time, and she said the books always came back.

She said I could help them every Saturday from now on. I was old enough to know what was going on and big enough to be helpful. We did it for several years. Jerry and I added a kids table and brought our favorite books along.

All of this happened in the late 1940's. The library was officially integrated when a new building opened in 1956, but the local history reports that Negroes were served long before that time.

Dark Water

I now know that I grew up in what is called the Jim Crow South. It had no such name then, though I do recall a song called *Jump Jim Crow*. It was a time rife with change that came slowly, tearing the fabric of custom and law, and changing the South, and indeed the country forever.

I knew early on that the people called "colored" lived differently from the ones I knew as "white." They ate different food, and the children were allowed to range farther across the creek and into the woods than we could. They could go outside barefoot, but I had to leave with my shoes on, and hide them next to a tree or in the creek bank once I got outside. I had no idea that their freedom was bogus, or that their living was less, until I went to school. Because I had a late fall birthday, I could not attend public school until I turned seven. Nor was I allowed to cross the busy street in front of our house. My world was a college campus where my brother and I played with the few other children who lived there too. We slipped off the grounds every now and then, being careful that Momma did not catch us. Our closest friend was Marshalljunior. He was a year older than my brother Jerry and five years older than me. He was colored, and could do things that we were not allowed to do, and he was my hero. I did not realize that we would not grow up together.

I recall one blistering July day when the world changed. It was shortly before my 7th birthday. My brother had turned 10 in May, and Marshall was 11. We had gone off to the shady woods and creek. It was forbidden territory, and I was scared. "We shouldn't be here," I said. "You know Momma's rule. Stay where we can hear her or we get into trouble. We're too far from home. We can't hear her. You know we can't. She'll spank us good. And we're never allowed at the creek. Not ever. I want to go home." I started to cry.

"Fraidy cat, Fraidy cat, don't be such a baby," teased Jerry. "Momma's gone to town, so she won't be hollering for us. Not till lunchtime. And the creek's gone dry, and anyway Marshalljunior's allowed to go the creek on account of he's colored. C'mon."

I looked at Marshalljunior. He said, "It's okay Missy, les just go down a little ways to the Blue Hole. They's water there still; it's just the creek bed what's dry. That pool, it's cool and deep. Might even see us a fish or two."

I wanted to go. The summer sun had burned down for weeks. It had soaked into the red earth, so we were pressed by heat from above and below. I was scared, and ashamed of being scared. I bit my cheek on the inside to keep from crying. "We can't hear Momma. I want to go home."

"So, go ahead. Don't let us stop you!" Jerry jeered. But I was scared to walk back through the woods by myself.

"No, you gotta come too. Let Marshalljunior go. He's allowed. We're not."

"Bye, bye, crybaby cry. Stick a finger in your eye. Just wait here by yourself then, Miss Goody Two Shoes." He started to walk off.

"Naw, we can't leave her," said Marshalljunior. "We're almost teenagers, and she's not even seven yet. C'mon Missy, it's not far. We'll cool off in that water for a minute or two, and then we'll run back so fast your Momma won't never know we left. You be settin on the porch swing when she come home."

So we stepped in the dry creek bed with our tough summer feet and picked our way over the rocks. I hurried to keep up. Marshaljunior was right; it wasn't far. The water at the swimming hole was still and dark, and the air felt thick. Nothing moved.

I put my toe in the pool, and Jerry said, "Dare you." And I said, "You go first. I double dog dare you!"

And while we stared at each other, Marshalljunior slipped off his dungarees and slid into the still water. I couldn't even see his legs, the water was so dark. There were goose bumps on his arms, and his teeth chattered. "Cool," he said. "Mighty fine! You comin, Missy?"

I looked around just to be sure nobody else was there. I pulled off my shirt and slipped in fast. Kept my shorts on because I was a girl. I could just barely touch bottom. "Beat you! Beat you!" I crowed and looked up at Jerry. He was standing stone still at the edge of the water. His skin was white under his tan, and he was pointing at something. His mouth was open, but he wasn't saying a word. Just pointing. "He's trying to scare me," I thought. "Now, who's the fraidy cat?" I hollered. Then I looked where he was pointing. I saw a triangle shaped black head on the end of what looked like a stick in the dark pool. It was near me....Nearer me....Nearer my God to Thee. I stopped breathing.

"Water moccasin," Jerry hissed. "Suky's brother died from just one bite."

"Stay still," Marshalljunior whispered, and he slid toward the head without making a ripple. The water around the snake bubbled the way it does before they strike. It turned its black eyes on me and fastened. Time stopped.

Marshalljunior's arm shot out and grabbed the moccasin up close behind its head. Its fangs were bare and quivering. Its tongue darted as it twisted and tried to strike. Marshalljunior squeezed it hard and then grabbed it farther down its backside with his left hand and squeezed harder. The snake flailed, and then it was still. Marshaljunior hurled it to the bank. It twitched as we watched, and then lay there shining in the sun with its eyes staring blankly.

We stood there still. Still as the snake. Stiller even. Waiting to see if it would come alive to coil and strike. We watched its shiny skin turn dull, as the sun beat down, hard and hot.

"Is it dead? I think it's dead," I whispered. Jerry broke off a long stick and poked it. It was black all over, even the underside. "It's dead okay, but don't touch it. It's still got poison; don't even go near," he said. "C'mon, we gotta go home."

We looked at each other. Marshalljunior without his jeans, his skinny black legs coming out of white underpants. Me with no shirt and my pink shorts all wet and stuck to my skin. Jerry still had his clothes on; his shirt was soaking wet with sweat. He tossed us our clothes. "Hurry up. We gotta get home before Momma."

We dried off as best we could and skinned back into our clothes. It was hard because we were wet. Nobody said anything as we picked our way back up the dry creek bed. We stopped at the edge of the woods. Looked each other over for changes.

"Look, there's no car in the driveway! Momma's not back yet," Jerry whispered. "We're home free."

"Praise Jesus!" Marshalljunior grinned.

"So we're not telling. Not any of us. Right?" said Jerry. "No squealing. Swear!"

"It's wrong to swear," I said. "I won't swear, but I promise I won't tell."

"No, you gotta swear. We all gotta swear," insisted Jerry. He smacked his tanned hand on Marshalljunior's black one and pressed mine on top. "Now! We won't, any of us, ever tell about going to the Blue Hole or about Marshalljunior killing the snake, or about anything that happened this whole entire morning. And we'll be blood buddies and stick by each other forever and ever. Swear it!

Really, Truly, Blackly, Bluely
Lay me down and Cut me Two-ly!

Say it now. Both of you. Say it. Say it twice."

So, Marshalljunior and I said it, and then we all three held hands in a circle and said it again just to make sure. "See you later then," said Marshalljunior. He looked at me. "You okay, Missy?" he asked. I nodded and he turned down the path toward his house.

"C'mon, we gotta get home," said Jerry. "Race you," he called to me over his shoulder as he kited toward our house. He won easily and shouted, "Beat you! Me first!"

"No fair, you got longer legs. You're sposed to give me a head start."

"You're lucky you still *got* legs," Jerry snarled. "If it wasn't for Marshalljunior…Remember now, no telling. You swore, and God'll get you if you break a swear."

We came up on the back porch and into the kitchen. There was Herculine, our day helper, pushing the iron over Poppa's handkerchiefs and singing one of her favorite songs. "*When I gets so old I can't dream anymore, I'll have you to remember me.*" She saw us and broke off her song. "Why bless your heart child. Look at you! You're all wet and muddy. Are you hurt? Where you been? What you children been up to?" She squatted down and held out her arms and folded me up to her.

"Shh," warned Jerry. "It's okay, Herc, she just fell down. Nothing to cry about. We're fine and we sure are hungry. Isn't it lunch time?"

"Why, sure it is," said Herculine. "Now you run and get cleaned up and I'll get your lunch out. Your Momma called and said she was meeting your Aunt Mary at Woolworths for a Coca Cola at the counter there. She said you should go ahead and eat."

"We made it," Jerry said as we went to our rooms. "Remember now, don't you tell anything. You swore."

"I won't," I said. I went to my room and took off my wet shorts. I hid them under the bed, hoping Momma wouldn't find them. She got mad when I had nightmares and wet my pants at night. Said I was too old for that kind of thing. I was too. She was right. But I didn't do it on purpose. I found some clean shorts in the drawer and went back to the kitchen.

Jerry and Herculine were out on the porch. Jerry was eating a cold fried chicken leg, and Herc was sitting on the glider drinking sweet tea. "Come here, Missy. Set here next to me and eat your lunch." She looked at me closely. "Maybe you could use a little nap after."

"Good idea!" Jerry jumped up. "I'm goin down to see Marshalljunior, Herc." He turned to me. "Don't you forget, Missy. Blackly, Bluely!" He ran his finger across his throat and took off down the steps.

I finished my chicken. "Do I have to have a nap, Herc? I'm kind of old for naps. Couldn't I maybe just sit and rock here on the glider with you?"

"Why yes, I reckon so," said Herc. She pulled me close to her and began to sing softly. "Jesus loves me, this I know, for the Bible tells me so."

"Does Jesus love everybody, Herc?"

"Yes indeed, child. Everybody in the whole wide world."

"Does he love us, even when we're bad?"

"Especially then, cause then is when we need him most."

"Even if we do bad things and lie about them?"

"Sure enough, but it makes him sad."

I told her then. The whole thing about how we went to the creek, even though we knew better and about the snake and how Marshalljunior killed it. "And we swore not to tell, and it's wrong to swear, and now I even broke my swear," I sobbed.

Herc pulled my head down on her lap and stroked my hair. "Hush baby, hush now." She started to hum.

I must have slept. The next thing I knew I was lying all by myself on the glider. There was a pillow under my head. The sun was low in the sky. Momma's car was in the driveway. I got up and found Herc in the kitchen, putting on her sun hat to go home.

"What am I gonna do, Herc? I broke my word to Jerry, and he'll be mad. And Momma's gonna spank me good too. Did you tell her what we did?"

Herc sat down and patted her lap. I crawled up and leaned my head against her. "You was sleeping when your momma come home. I told her you had a bad, bad dream about snakes and you was mighty scared. She said you had probably heard that story about Suky's brother getting bit. I said I reckoned that might be so. Jerry was standing right there and heard it all. He didn't say a word."

She set me down on the floor, stood up and put on her hat. Before she left, she took my face and held it in both of her hands the way she always did when she wanted to be sure I paid attention. She looked me right in the eyes. "I expect neither one of you be going back to that Blue Hole any time soon."

Back Home

"Flight Attendants prepare for landing." I jerk awake. It is Friday evening. I have decided to fly to Atlanta directly after my workday in Boston in order to spend as much time as I can with Daddy. I make the trip often. It is what I have to give, and it is never enough to fill his loneliness. I love my father. I love my three sons and my husband. My job with a newly up and running hospice is immensely challenging and satisfying. I do very little in my life that I don't want to do, and it still adds up to more time than there is in the day, the week, the month. Too many blessings, I admit ruefully. I tell myself that these are designer problems, and I am lucky to have them. But I often feel remiss. The "shoulds" take up a lot of space. A lot of me.

The landing gear locks into place. Looking out the window, I see the city sprawled below in a vast milky way of lights. I remember my first plane trip to Atlanta when I was a young teen, nearly a quarter of a century ago. I had been invited to take part in a statewide high school conference with my idol, Elizabeth Ansley, who was president of the senior class. I could probably have flown from the thrill of that alone. The flight from La Grange, Georgia, had taken twenty minutes. We exited the plane right onto the runway, with both of our Daddies standing there on the tarmac to meet us. A time gone by for sure.

Gathering my own gear of brief case, small bag, and a box of cigars for Daddy, I make my way past the gate. I do not expect anyone to meet me. Daddy doesn't drive anymore and Momma has been gone for five years...nearly six now. I know that I'll never stop missing her. I reach into my pocket for the exact change for MARTA, the rapid transit train. It would speed across Atlanta to Daddy's stop in just 20 minutes. "Faster than a speeding bullet," I smile wryly, recalling the old radio description of Superman. I remember lying on the floor and staring at the single yellow light on the radio cabinet, listening. Friday evenings. Seven o'clock.

This trip is always hard. As the city has grown modern, my father has grown old. His apartment smells of closed up old man and stale cigars. The kitchen is never quite clean. It holds the droppings of an old man who still cooks his own meals and sets the table to eat them alone. He cleans up afterwards, in his fashion, leaving toast crumbs on the floor and bacon grease in the pan. His graying underwear hangs drying on a rack in the warm corner of the pantry. He fades from one visit to the next. I miss Momma. The trips back are bittersweet reminders of lives that have changed, diminished, ended. I miss being young.

I get to the edge of the moving sidewalk and follow the signs for MARTA. In less than two minutes the train slides quietly into the station. I pass through the doors, not realizing that a shadow of the little girl I'd once been would board the train with me, that the train would travel back in time as it moved forward in space.

I should have been prepared for her. That little girl often turned up on these trips, usually in some old haunt, or in the smell of biscuits baking. She had been called Betsy Holland, in the Southern fashion of using double names. I outgrew her a long time ago. She is a fearful, self-righteous brat. She is also a piece of my history.

The train is crowded. I find a seat, store my bag underneath and begin to look around the car. There are the usual ads…a transit map, a glittering poster of *Underground Atlanta*. I shake my head at the poster that screams "**SINNERS WANTED**" in neon purple lettering. There is a Bible verse underneath and the hours for services at a church near Grant Park where **All are Welcome**. Below it I see an ad for a car rental company that offers pick up and delivery service. The office is in the mall near Daddy's apartment.

I jot down the phone number.

I wonder if he'd like to go out. It would break up his relentless litany of small daily tasks and perhaps bring back pleasant memories. We usually just walk around the neighborhood when I come and chat with a few folks out with their dogs. Daddy claims that walking is good for him but on my last trip here I noticed that it taxed his joints. And it took a great toll on my reserves of patience. My usual stance in life is to appear calm and unruffled. My brother Jerry teases me that I burn a lot of calories that way. But he knows me well. Most people don't see down to that part, and I don't go out of my way to show them.

If Daddy agrees to the car rental idea, we can drive to his old favorite restaurant where the headwaiter will probably remember him and his favorite German beer and pastrami sandwich. It is an easy drive to Fulton Street, and that neighborhood is still safe. Then on Sunday we might go to church and visit his old Sunday school class— the one he and Momma taught for so many years. He goes there now only when someone can drive across town to pick him up. He and the class have diminished together. He says it will probably die when he does, and I guess he may be right. But at least he'd see an old friend or two—feel part of something again. He might remember Momma in the days when her warm heart and grasshopper mind brightened the planet. Her dwindling had taken so long that it was sometimes hard to recall her wonderful laughter and quick tongue. Hard to remember the delight she took in the world and brought to it.

Daddy says that her absence remains a dull hole in the sky where a bright star used to be. His memory of her is constant and bittersweet.

My two days back home begin to hold some promise. I relax a little and look at the faces around me. They are all varying shades of black and brown, but definitely what as a child, I had known as "colored." I realize that I am the only white person in the car. That little girl in me so clearly remembers the "back of the bus" stuff of my childhood. Memories start cascading – how proud I was not so long ago when my brother went to Selma and got himself arrested. I recall the faces of the neighboring children who were my friends before I started school and discovered that they were not allowed there. I cried for a while, but I got over it and made new friends, just the way my big sister Meg told me I would. I remember how angry I felt then, reacting with the purity that children lose so quickly.

The train passes familiar landmarks: the Varsity, Georgia Tech, and the gold dome of the capitol. It stops for several minutes at Grant Field where the ball game has just ended. More people crowd on. I watch the sneaker-footed riders who are laughing and shoving good-naturedly. The Braves have won in extra innings and the night is pleasant.

Most of the riders are men. Some have brought their children, mostly sons, who lean tiredly or are hyper with the excitement of being out so late on a Friday night. It is a happy crowd, and people are joking and chattering with each other. Black, every one of them. No one pays the slightest attention to me. I feel myself growing smaller every second, and whiter. I feel like a little kid again, but no one seems to notice.

"*We're on the wrong train!*" The voice of the little girl takes me by surprise. It's Betsy Holland's voice. "*This is not our train. Everyone is colored.*"

I push the voice out of my head. "*Get lost,*" I tell her, but she goes on. "*I'm scared.*"

"*Nonsense, we're on our way to Daddy's house. There's nothing to be afraid of.*"

"*I'm scared,*" she repeats, "*I don't belong here.*"

I know this conversation isn't real. It's what Momma called a daymare. She had them too, and said you just had to be quiet and wait them out. Still, I begin to look about with some uncertainty. Then I squeeze my eyes shut and hold my breath. The train speeds on. People get on and off, mostly off, exulting in the victory of the Braves. It's their ball club...and my ball club too.

The transit voice crackles on: "Peachtree/Piedmont, next stop. Please wait for the train to stop and stay away from the moving doors." I open my eyes. Oh good, my stop.

I'm just a short block from Daddy's apartment. I know he will be waiting up for me.

I reach down for my bag. "That looks kinda heavy, Ma'am." I look up into a light brown teen-aged face. "I'll carry it up for you." The young man has a Braves cap on backwards, a red tank top, and a silver cross around his neck. I look around the train. Only half filled now, and pretty quiet. He smiles, and I notice his white teeth and his long hair tightly braided.

His offer is clear. Everyone must have heard it. No one looks alarmed or even much interested. He reaches for my bag. A stab of fear twists in me. I tighten my grip on the strap. "Oh, it's not heavy, thanks anyway." I hear myself say politely.

"Aw, it's okay, this is my stop too." His dark hand closes on the strap, right next to my white one.

I can almost hear Betsy Holland whimpering, *"He's gonna run off with our bag. You know he is. He'll get ahead of us on those stairs, and then he'll take off like a shot. Tell him, No Thank You."*

For an instant, I merge with the child. I feel nauseous. There is no air on the train.

"Hey, Ma'am, are you okay?" He comes a step closer. My vision blurs and grows crinkly around the edges. "Ma'am?"

I make it back. "Oh, goodness, where are my manners?" Loosing my grip on the bag and looking up at him, I say, "Thank you." We walk up the stairs together.

He sets the bag down at the top of the stairs and disappears into the night. There is no sound from Betsy Holland. She has disappeared into the world where she grew up.

I take a deep breath, shoulder my bag and begin to walk the short block down the well-lighted street to Daddy's apartment. I pass the Seven-Eleven Store and a couple of people out with their dogs. I wonder what Daddy would think about my experience on the train. Will I tell him about it? He knows about Momma's daymares. The trained psychologist in him would find it interesting, but the fragile old man might be fearful. I feel protective. I'll decide that one tomorrow. Right now I'm bone tired. I remember Momma's sister, Aunt Gracious, saying that tired children should not make decisions. She had no children of her own, and not much patience.

Daddy is indeed awake. I can see the porch light shining like a beacon. He makes sure his world is lighted clearly all the time. He still holds the fears of a ragged childhood, moving to a different town, a different house and a different school year after year when the summer music season ended. He acquired asthma, and an abiding dislike of dark streets, poverty, and new places. Defying his experience, he became a settled and successful academic, but he has never shaken the memories.

I see him peering through the two-way window as my foot hits the front steps. The double locks click, and suddenly he is standing in the doorway, with his arms wide open. "Ah, you are a fine sight for the eyes of this old man," he grins and holds his arms out for a hug. "I've greeted every car and every dog that passed by the apartment in the last hour! And now, here you are!" He is tired, but clearly relieved and happy to see me. As we hug in the small entrance, I notice that he is more stooped than before…and thin. "I brought you cigars," I say, handing him a box that says *Roi-Tan*. "I hope they are decent. We can't get *Hav-a-Tampas* any more."

"I know," he replies. "The Cuban embargo is ridiculous. Hurts everyone and helps no one. And I do miss those fine cigars!" He sets the box down on the table by his chair. I notice that there are two place mats on the dining table in honor of my arrival, and a small vase of pansies. They were Momma's favorite flowers, and I was always allowed to pick as many as I wanted.

The place looks picked up though it smells like dead cigars. In the old days he smoked two cigars a day, and only outside, then flushed the butts down the toilet so there would be no odor in the house. Momma objected to the smell and he was careful. They got on well in a marriage of more than fifty years. He took care of her at home for as long as he could when her mind began to leave her, and visited her in the nursing home every day for her last two years on earth. He packed his bags when she died and the time since has been mostly about waiting to go himself. I notice that his corduroy robe has stains that he can no longer see, and his slippers have holes in the soles. I'll send new ones as soon as I get back home. Long feet, size 13. The apartment looks pretty much the same. Books stacked by the Barcalounger and the current *New Yorker* on the table. A half glass of something that once held ice sits idly by.

"Would you like a drink before bed?" he asks, looking down wistfully at the glass on the table.

"No thanks," I say. "I'm weary. I went to the airport straight from work, so it's been a long day. I talked with Jerry this morning though, and I'll tell you about it first thing in the morning." I can see that he does not want to go to bed yet, so I add, "Jerry sounds fine. You know, he is as good as a brother could be." I can see he is hanging on my words. "We both wish we lived closer to you." And I go on to say what I've said before about his moving to Boston near us, or to the Carolina Mountains where Jerry lives with his kids.

He half smiles. "Well, I don't know about moving. But your Momma is buried up there in those mountains and she loved to walk through the woods. Maybe she still does. I wonder." He turns to lead the way upstairs. I notice that his gait is slow and he holds the rail tightly.

My little room looks about the same. Neat and almost completely without character. A cotton bedspread in place of Grandmother's old quilt, and plastic blinds instead of curtains. I can feel Momma's absence. Daddy moved here to be near the nursing home when he could no longer care for her at home. She had lost her strong quick mind and could not find it again. She began to wander physically and mentally, becoming a cruel parody of her sturdy self.

The twin bed from my childhood still has a teddy bear though, and Daddy has added a framed photo of Momma since the last time I was here. It's a studio portrait that could be almost anybody. It does catch her large nose—Roman—she called it. But it misses all of her brightness and warmth. I try to reconstruct her image but I'm too tired. I can almost hear her saying, "Tomorrow is another day. Rest now, little one." I close my eyes and mercifully find no dreams waiting.

Daddy wakes with the sun as he always has. He's in the tiny kitchen and I hear him humming an old cowboy song. *"I ride an old Paint, I lead an old Dan."* He sang us a song each night after Momma told an Uncle Remus story or read from *Alice in Wonderland* or *The Wind in the Willows*. Bedtimes were comfortable times and I tried to recreate them for my children. Most nights we read a story and sang a song. Their favorite was *Wynken, Blynken, and Nod*. I still know every word.

I make my way downstairs and help myself to Daddy's strong coffee. Two big gulps and I broach the subject of the rental car. "Daddy, I found out that there's a rental car place at the mall down the street. They'll pick us up and manage the paper work right here on the spot. Wouldn't it be fun to get out for a bit? We could drive out to Stone Mountain, or do your errands, or visit an old friend or two."

I thought he might be fearful, but after a few seconds he says, "Well, that might just be a fine idea. I thought you could only rent cars at the airport, and I knew I didn't want you making that drive… ten lanes on each side, turning off and on, and going way too fast. Are you sure there's a place close by?" He adds, "You know what I'd really like to do is to visit the Haven. It feels strange that I don't get there any more. I never missed a day in all the years your Momma lived there. Not even one." He is proud and rightly so. "And on Saturdays I played the piano in the big hall. All the residents gathered in the circle of chairs and sang. Funny, they didn't know what day it was, or sometimes even who they were. But they knew every word of those war songs: *Lili Marlene, Over There*. And the campground hymns: *Do Lord* and *I Come to the Garden Alone*, the pop songs, the show tunes." He breaks into a round of *Daisy, Daisy, give me your answer true*. "They may not remember me, but they'll know those old songs for sure. And maybe they'll smile for just a little while." He has slipped back in time. I wish he could stay there.

He comes back. "And maybe for a minute, you'll have a bit of your old Daddy back instead of this shuffling old man. And a memory of your Momma. It will be almost like going home to me."

I cringe inside at our very different memories of the nursing home but I smile as brightly as I can. Yes, I can do this.

He goes on. "Do you remember that restaurant, the Roundabout, where we used to go? It was not too far from the Haven. If it is still there, we might have a nice lunch after the Haven. I'd love a martini and maybe a nap. We could just have pancakes and bacon for supper." I see the beginning of a smile.

I grin back at him. "Sure, and then we could also think about going somewhere on Sunday. My plane is not until 2:00. We could maybe go to your old church in Druid Hills or out to see what became of the high school in Decatur. Jerry told me it has been totally rebuilt. Or even to Stone Mountain." I find myself nervously fingering my coffee cup. "I have vivid memories of all those places. Funny, Druid Hills was safe because it had Bible stories and hymns. But Stone Mountain was so scary. That was where the Klu Klux Klan did all its terrible stuff." I want to know the expression on his face, but can't look. "But I hear it is a national park now, and it might be interesting to go out there."

I see that Daddy is not paying attention to my prattle about tomorrow. His mind is fixed on the Haven. He smiles gently and says, "So let's see about that car. It sure is good to have you back home," adding wryly, "at least what there is left of back home."

I call the car rental company, and a driver turns up in minutes. We drive back to the agency a few blocks away, passing two car washes, a Burger King, and four gas stations. The rental process is simple and we are on our way to the Haven within half an hour. I am aware all over again of the familiar sinking feeling that used to come with these visits. Momma was there but not there. Her Irish blue eyes no longer sparkling, her smiles tentative…a "please like me" look from her once confident, vibrant face. The low brick structure looks neat amid the tidy evergreens, and the marigolds along the concrete drive are bright. We park easily, right near the bench where Daddy used to smoke his cigar after each visit. The front desk is unattended. Visitors are not expected this early.

We take ourselves to the big hall. It is even drearier than I remembered. Badly lighted. Not quite clean. A few people share the vinyl sofa, and some are still seated in the chairs where they had breakfast and will remain for lunch. The tables have been washed down. Wheelchairs line the walls and the air is spray smell sweet. My heart sinks but Daddy is at his best. The complete gentleman, going round the room chair-by-chair, shaking the hands of blank eyed folks and getting an occasional smile in return.

He stops to greet a shriveled, frail, colored woman who is trying to turn her wheel chair. "Here, Mrs. Wellman," he says, "Let me help

you with that." He turns her chair so that it faces the door to the hall. She rewards him with a radiant smile. "Oh thank you," she says. "I'm sure Mr. Wellman will be coming right along any minute, as soon as his train gets in. He's a porter on the Southern Railway, you know. He won't forget me.

Why, he might even be here before lunch."

I remember Mrs. Wellman. She was here all those years ago when Momma came, and she's been watching that door with complete trust ever since. Daddy smiles and shakes her hand. "Well, I know he is mighty eager to see you," he says.

He moves on over to the upright piano and settles on the bench. He plays by ear and leads the singing easily. One man asks for *The Old Rugged Cross*, all the verses please. Then the tiny woman next to him quavers into *Madam, Miss Otis Regrets*, but mercifully gives out at the fifth verse. Even Daddy doesn't remember all the words. I recall that she regrets missing her luncheon engagement because she is being executed at high noon for shooting and killing her lover. But the lyrics escape me too. So many old songs: *Take Me Out to the Ball Game*, *I'm Forever Blowing Bubbles*, *Look Down That Lonesome Road*. The room begins to come alive as the trays roll in – canned corn and something that might be meat loaf. It is their lunchtime and ours. I am relieved. We can leave.

We sanitize our hands as we exit the building and return to the car to make our way toward lunch. It is not far, and Walter, the waiter, does indeed remember Daddy even after all this time. He suggests a martini and Daddy is delighted. I realize that he has probably had more conversation in these few hours than in all of the previous month. He speaks of the people we saw, one by one. I remember only Mrs. Wellman from the past and I am touched by how real and dear they each have remained to him. The restaurant is noisy with three televisions blaring different sporting events and the "regulars" making bets. Daddy seems happy with his drink and sandwich and is more than willing to return to the apartment for a nap. I find that I am weary as well. Once he is settled, I slip off to my little room to catch up on my staring, a practice I developed years ago. Just looking out the window and not thinking is more restorative than sleeping or reading.

Over pancakes that evening we look back together. Daddy has another martini – the second of the day. I have a twinge of fear as I wonder how much he may be drinking at home alone. I take myself in hand and remember that he is 80 years old, not driving, and it is none of my business. He's quite talkative. Both the alcohol and the simple presence of someone who will listen fuel him. He recalls the pleasure that Momma got from the sing-along each week. "Why, she knew the words to everything," he says, "especially the hymns. She could belt out *Rock of Ages*, all the verses, and *I Come to the Garden*. I never let her know how much I didn't like that one. Schmaltzy and saccharine. But she'd loved it from her childhood Bible School." I grin and start to sing it:

> "I come to the garden alone,
> While the dew is still on the roses
> And the voice I hear falling on my ear
> The Son of God discloses.
> And He walks with me, and He talks with me,
> and tells me I am His own."

Daddy covers his ears and I laugh. I realize again that we remember Momma and the Haven very differently. I mostly remember how lost and frightened and shrunken she was then, and how helpless I felt as I watched her mind depart and her anxiety increase. He recalls her sweetness and his own ability to help her in her sad aging.

"Did going there today bring back even younger memories of her?" I ask. Sadness comes to his eyes. "Oh, yes," he says, "but I don't want to hold on to them because

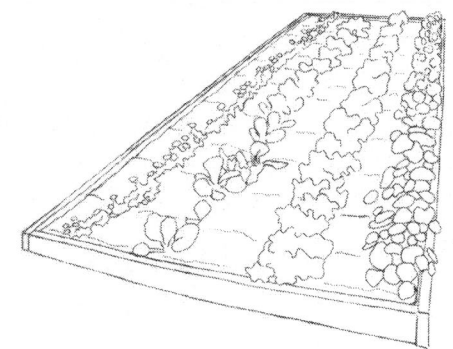

-

they make me miss her even more." Then he risks thinking back. "Do you remember when you were little, maybe about 5 or 6? Dr. Blakely, the president of the college wanted your momma to have a rose garden next to the house? It was a shabby little house and he thought to pretty it up. You know, make the Dean's house look good. It was during the War, maybe 1942 or 1943. Your Momma wanted a Victory Garden instead, but he said no. He thought that would be undignified. His secretary went ahead and ordered the dirt, not knowing that it would come from a vegetable farm. It was good, rich black dirt, and before she could even order the rose plants, little tomatoes began to sprout up. Your Momma, bless her heart, put on her Sunday best and went over to the president's office. She turned on her sweetest charm and told him about the tomatoes. She said it would be unpatriotic to pull them out in favor of roses, what with the war going on. She was sure the garden would make a fine statement for the college. Well, Dr. Blakely was not nearly as quick as your Momma, and he gave in. We had a whopping garden that year and the next year too. Beans and tomatoes. Do you remember? I was so proud of her."

I laughed. I had wonderful warm memories of standing out in that garden with my brother Jerry. We popped those tiny baby tomatoes in our mouths like candy and stood there grazing till somebody made us come away.

We return to the present. He asks kindly about my sons. They are nearly grown now. The youngest, Andrew, is in his teens. Ted is in his last year at the Latin School and headed for college next year. George needed some more growing up time and joined the US Navy. Probably a good move for him, though we worry. Andrew has his own band and is becoming a fine guitar player. "Like his Grandfather before him," I smile, as Daddy adds "and his Great Grandfather too." He smiles as he thinks back, "Yes," he says, "you all grew up on songs. Now your Grandfather. ...music wasn't all fun and games for him. He ran away from home when he was 16." Daddy goes on to tell me about how his father could play any horn there was and that he lied about his age so he could join the army during the Spanish/American War. He was too young to fight, but he played the fife and drums and led the troops as they marched. "He came home when he was twenty, with malaria, tuberculosis and a determination to make a life in music. He did too. I grew up in orchestra pits, with a wide assortment of people, some of them pretty unsavory. I reckon it left a mark. Hope that your Andrew moves toward the concert hall or the high tone clubs if he stays with the guitar. He might make a decent living playing classical guitar these days."

He looks at me closely. "We tried to give you three a stable childhood," he said. "Course the country was just coming out of the Depression and then there was the War.

Nobody had money but we got along. The college campus was a good place to bring up children. And by the time we left there and moved to Decatur, your sister was on her way to college, and your brother was well into high school. I guess you were the one who had to adapt the most." I see him working to put the pieces together. "How old were you? I can't remember. Maybe twelve or so?"

"That was 1950, the summer I turned twelve." I replied lightly, but I remembered well. Daddy had a new job where he was going to do *very important things*. Nobody explained to me what these things were. All I knew was that Daddy traveled, and Momma went back to work. Who knew what would happen to me? And did anybody care?

My parents decided that I would travel with Daddy in the old green Hudson that summer. Momma gave me a little notebook to record my trip. I couldn't imagine what I might want to write. I didn't even want to be there. Days in the car were long and noisy and hot. There was no point in looking out the window to count cows, or to look for graveyards without my brother there to compete. And I wasn't all that comfortable with Daddy anyway. What could we talk about? And when we got wherever we were going, day after hot day, there was no place for me. Everybody else was colored. I was extra. The wrong age and the wrong color.

We never spent the night with people who lived on the campus we were visiting. Out of town folks had always stayed at our house, so that felt strange to me. Sometimes we stayed in a motel with a swimming pool. I liked to swim and so that sort of helped, but I felt awkward too. My beginning- to- change body embarrassed me. I hoped Daddy wouldn't tease me or look at me or say anything. He sometimes watched me out of the corner of his eye and made comments about my growing up, and I wanted to disappear. I guess he thought he was being funny, or hip, or something! I watched carefully for the chance to slip into the bathroom unnoticed and change into my bathing suit and cover myself completely with a big shirt.

I recall one of our trips to a college in South Carolina. "Do you remember Spartanburg, Daddy? While you were off working, I spent the day with the Dean's wife and her little daughter Patty Lee. She had tiny braids all over her head. I think she was about seven or eight, and she was kind of shy. Seemed nice but really young. It was a long day. And so hot! I thought you'd never turn up. Finally around three o'clock you came. I had what I thought was a great idea. When we drove into town the night before, I'd noticed that the movie Snow White was playing on Main Street, not far away. It was my favorite movie. I'd seen it five times already and was shooting for ten. My friend Leah had seen it a dozen times. I knew we had a couple of hours before supper, and so I asked if we could take Patty Lee to see the movie. Maybe her mother would like to come too? I thought it was a really nice invitation, but nobody answered me. Not a word. Do you remember, Daddy? You just frowned and shook your head at me, as Patty Lee said, 'Oh, yes, please. I've never been to a movie. Please can we go?' Her mom looked at you, not me or Patty, and said, 'Well, maybe someday.'

It was awkward and I knew I'd done something wrong, but I didn't know what. The movie would have been fun, and it would be polite to do something nice for Patty Lee, who had spent all that long hot day entertaining me. We left awkwardly. When we got back to the car, you explained to me that colored people could not go to the movies with white people unless there was a separate balcony upstairs where they could sit. There was only one theater in this town, and it had no balcony. There was no way I could take Patty Lee to the movies. The movie theater was for white folks. No balcony. No Negroes. I was stunned."

Looking at Daddy now, I shake my head. "There was so much I didn't know. I know now that you were leading the way toward college integration in the South. There wasn't a black college where you were not beloved or feared, or both. All I knew was that I didn't want to be there. Why didn't you tell your kids what it was all about? We weren't babies. We could have understood. It would have made sense of the whole, hard move to Atlanta." My voice has risen an octave. I can hear its shrillness.

He looks at me a long time. He is close to angry. "You just don't get it. Your mother and I wanted to protect you. It turned out that most of my recommendations on accreditation were accepted quietly. Improving anyone's education was deemed a good thing for a while. Neither your mother nor I ever went to the press or took a public stand. We voted with our lives and our actions."

I try to explain. "But we were your children, not the public. We got moved with you. We deserved to know why. You and Momma underestimated us."

"Maybe you are right," he says more calmly "but with the information we had at the time, we made the best decision we could."

I put down my end of the rope. This conversation is done, probably overdone. In a conciliatory tone I add, "Well I'm proud to know you."

He stands and almost bows. "Same back at you," he replies. And with that we head up the stairs to bed. It's been a long day.

Sleep is a long way off. Images pile up in my head like early movies without sound. I am stuck in the early 1950's remembering life as young teenager in a new place. Home was changing. Meg was away at college. Daddy traveled a lot, and I got used to having him gone. Momma was out all day teaching. Jerry and I were both at the upper school, grades 7-12. I remember the long walk to get there, the awkwardness of changing clothes for gym, the smell of disinfectant, the noise of the football games and the flaming red of the Latin teacher's dyed hair.

I can see the place clearly as I lie here in bed. Three brick buildings with their names carved in stone in the middle of each. Decatur Boys High School and Decatur Girls High School on each end, and Recreation Building for the lunchroom and the gymnasium in the middle. The football stadium and playing field stretched out behind the buildings and backed up to the fence at the edge of colored town. The fence was low and the gate was never locked. Kids from there wandered over to our field after school every day. We all knew each other and got along fine. The time of troubles was soon to follow, but had not openly begun yet.

Football was king, and my brother Jerry was our star defensive back. I was proud of him, and I'd go with other girls to watch the practices. I dreamed of being a cheerleader. As my thoughts drift back, I remember that Jerry used to lose several footballs each week by clumsy practice passes over the fence and into colored town. At first I felt bad for him, and then I saw that no one cared. Coach Mike just tossed out another ball. 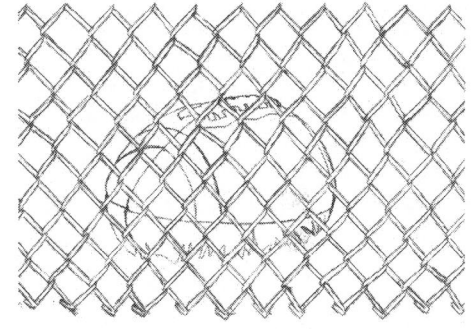 He'd say, "Oh let it go, son. That ball will find a receiver for sure." I finally realized that Jerry was losing the balls on purpose so that the colored kids would find them, and that Coach Mike knew it too. But I never asked, and no one ever said a word. I drift off to sleep with the arc of the football going over the fence.

I wake slowly in the morning to the smell of bacon and coffee and burnt toast. I find Daddy settled at the table with his breakfast and the *Atlanta Constitution*. He's dressed in a warm plaid shirt and looks ready to go out. It's a beautiful fall morning. He proposes a ride out to Decatur where we used to live. Ever the careful planner, he observes that the roads will be clear on a Sunday morning and we can be out there in no time. Maybe we could find our old house and it would be interesting to take a look at the new high school. It is not far and he remembers the way. We get there quickly. The town has mushroomed, becoming part of Greater Atlanta. I have no idea how to find our house in the suburban spread, but we make our way easily to the high school. Colored town is gone, replaced by a huge stadium and gym complex. A string of modern connected buildings wanders over the space where white boys and white girls were once schooled separately. No black children anywhere in those days. I feel left out in time. Erased, except for memories. We drive to the town square, and I am relieved to see that the old courthouse with its historic hitching posts for horses is still in place. There is some continuity at least.

"It's time for a second breakfast," Daddy says, "and then we can decide what to do next. We'll need to keep track of your time. The Atlanta airport is big, you know. They tell you to get there two hours early." I smile to myself, knowing that any argument will be useless. We park at the Courthouse and cross the street to Effie's Café, one of the few old businesses still around the square. The once green Formica counters have lost their shine and the vinyl stools have cracks. There are no lattes or espressos but the doughnuts glisten with sugar, and the menu claims to have grits. Daddy shakes his head. "I didn't know places had grits any more. Your Momma hated them. Said they were tasteless and low class. I'll never forget the day I went to see her at the Haven, and there she sat, bib around her neck, wolfing down grits with butter." He smiles wistfully.

"That's when I knew she was truly gone."

We order coffee and a doughnut each. I can see that Daddy has made a decision. He clears his throat. "I appreciate your offer to go to church," he says, "but I don't think I'm up for seeing those folks today. I like to let them know a week ahead if I'm coming. Then they plan for me. I know so few of them anymore. It just feels awkward. The class is smaller now, and at least half of the present members never even knew your Momma."

"That sounds hard. How about we take a ride out to Stone Mountain instead? I'd be interested in seeing it again--besides it's a pretty day for a drive."

"All right," he says. "I've heard that it's totally changed. The Tennant family that owned it and allowed the Klan to do its dirty business out there--they sold it to the state. It's a park now with amusements and picnic tables and restaurants." He takes a deep breath. "I heard there were rides too, and a cable car." I can see he is thinking back. "Who would ever have thought that would happen in a place that saw such awful things?'"

"Maybe you did, " I answer.

"What do you mean?"

"You never let us go there when we were growing up. I thought it must be a very awful place, and I was afraid." I'm aware of my throat tightening. "There was no television then, and even the newspapers were pretty quiet. We knew that it was dangerous out there, and we knew that the danger was people."

Daddy frowns and clears his throat. "Well...I guess we'd better go see it," he says. We get back in the car. "Tell me what you remember."

I back out and head for the interstate. "Well, there weren't so many buildings and highways back then. But even so, we could not see the mountain clearly from out here in Decatur in the daytime. It was different in the dark." As I say this, I notice billboards for cars and food are now blocking the view. Signs for Toshiba and Toyota loom up on the side of the road, followed by Burger King. A *See Atlanta* tourist sign points downtown and the Fox Theater is just one exit away. The city has spread into one vast metropolis. There is an advertisement for Stone Mountain Park, but the mountain itself remains hidden.

Memory kicks in with surprising urgency. "I remember one particular night in the summer -- I never told you and Momma about it. I was afraid you'd be angry at me."

"Would you tell me now?" he asks. I can't read his voice, but I hear the strain. I'm glad we are driving-- easier talking when we don't have eye contact. Both our parents had stonewalled us whenever we asked about the Stone Mountain.

" I was twelve. We had all gone to bed -- the house was dark. I woke up for no particular reason. That happened sometimes, and I usually went back to sleep pretty fast.

But this time as I looked out of the window, I saw bright light flickering in the distance. It was way off toward the mountain and I could tell it was not electric by the way it moved around. It had to be fire. I sneaked out to the kitchen and got Jerry's field glasses—the ones he took when he went hiking—and brought them back to my room. I was never supposed to touch them, but I told myself I'd be very careful and remember to put them back right away. I held them steady and managed to focus on the light. There were three shapes that looked like crosses on what had to be the top of Stone Mountain. One big cross was in the middle, taller than the others by a long way. There were white shapes, lots of them, moving around on the ground near them. I couldn't tell what they were; they were very small next to the crosses, but they were clearly alive."

Daddy looks over at me. "Go on," he says, his voice sounding crumbly and suddenly old, "or do you want to pull over?

"No," I say, "I'm okay and I'd like to tell you about this before we get there and see how the mountain looks all these years later ---see it in the daylight."

"Okay, if you are sure," he says.

"I was so scared," I say, "but I couldn't move. I knew I was not supposed to be awake, or using Jerry's glasses. So I just held my breath and kept looking. I remembered from Sunday School that when Jesus was crucified, there were three crosses - one for him and two for the thieves on either side. So I thought something like that must be happening again. I just sat there, still and terrified. The blaze finally died down. I guess I went back to sleep, but I remember asking in the morning about the fires in the night. You and Momma said I must have had a bad dream. I knew that wasn't true, but I couldn't say my parents were lying."

Daddy is silent, then nods his head.

" Jerry just looked at me and didn't say a word," I say. "He shook his head and put his finger on his lips to signal me to be quiet. Later he told me there was a lot of stuff going on out there that we weren't supposed to know about and that I should leave it alone. He said he had sneaked out there a couple of times in the daytime when his friend Tommy had the car to do errands for his Mom. They had seen the burned out fire sites. I asked if there were crosses, and he said no, not any more. But he could see that there had been. He said we'd best just stay clear of it all. I asked if you and Momma knew about it, and he said he reckoned you did. But he didn't plan on asking, and I'd be smart to keep my mouth shut too."

The sound of the road comes up to me, steady and relentless.

" I know now that those white shapes were hooded men, and that the crosses were a warning from the Klu Klux Klan. I don't know how I found out. You certainly didn't tell us, and it wasn't news in the *Atlanta Constitution* the next day. But I heard some kids at school talking."

I turn to look at him. "Didn't you and Momma know what was going on?" My voice is shrill again. "You must have known. You didn't trust us?" I hear my anger and am surprised by it. Nothing will be gained by scolding this old man. Not now.

Daddy heard me correctly. His voice cracks. "We wanted to protect you. We couldn't know what was actually happening, but we knew for sure that we didn't want you children getting curious and going out there. Especially Jerry. He was a hothead. He had friends with cars, and you would follow him anywhere on heaven or earth…even to Stone Mountain! We were trying to keep you safe."

It's the same theme I heard yesterday, and I nearly sink my teeth into it. But I stop. This is old history. A rest stop is coming up and I pull into it. "Let's stretch our legs. I need a break."

We walk along a circular path ringed by small trees. Daddy tries to explain—he wants to make it all right. "I'm proud of all of you— of what you did. Your brother went off to Selma and got himself arrested. You heard Thurgood Marshall in New Orleans and raced off to register black voters when you were at Tulane." I feel him being pushed by tides of history and parenting. " And your sister! She marched in Cumming where Andrew Young and Hosea Williams led that march of over 10,000 people, in total silence while the KKK stood by on the road and heckled....even Coretta Scott King was there."

"I remember that. Meg said she just loved to march, and she did a lot of it. She went all over the county. I always felt I didn't quite measure up. Later, she said she'd send her kids through the school picket lines to support integration. I wasn't sure what choice I'd make if it came to that. I was glad I didn't have kids! I knew that if I did have them, I'd want to keep them safe, but I'd also want them to go to school and learn to read. Meg was so sure of herself."

"Always has been...she doesn't see grays," Daddy says, "Just barrels right ahead."

We pick up a flyer for the Stone Mountain Park as we walk by the information booth and head back to the car. The air between us has cleared a little. Daddy rests his hand on my shoulder. It is just a short drive now to the parking lot.

We pull in and are stunned. A vast Disneyland sprawls before us. Here, where bigots in white once terrorized the population, there rises a gigantic carving in the granite mountain of Jefferson Davis, Stonewall Jackson, and Robert E. Lee, all mounted on massive steeds. They look down at the site where crosses used to burn. Below them we see a roller coaster, and a merry go round, whirling swings, and a tilt-a-whirl. Fast food vendors call to us. Above us sprawls a man-made snowfield for skiing.

As we get out of the car, we notice a cable car that runs all the way from this parking lot up to the three Confederate heroes. Images of past and present collide as we stand there: the white robes, the fires and the crosses all darkening the glittering façade of the amusement park. And the cable car? I ask Daddy if he'd like to ride up. He says he can't think of anything he'd rather not do. Then he suggests we walk up the mountain to the heroes. I know the climb will be too hard for him and wonder what he really wants to do and what he wants to say.

I see him hesitate. I wonder if we just might talk across the years.

But he retreats. Looks at his watch again and says, "Oh no, it is too late. You'll miss your flight unless we start back soon."

"There is a later flight," I offer. "It's not till evening. I could take that one." I reach for my cell phone.

"Would you really do that?" he says, his eyes brightening. "Your family's expecting you."

I think he may be about to let me in, to talk about what really happened all those years ago and how it was for him and Momma. "You bet I would, " I say forcefully.

Tears come to his eyes. He hesitates, then blinks them away. The moment passes. He is *The Father* again. "No, I think you'd best be off." He turns and walks toward the car. I follow, a little relieved but very sad. We came so close.

"Wait a minute!" I grab his arm. "This matters. Can we just finish this conversation?" I see him hesitate, and I add without thinking, "I love you."

His face breaks open. " And I love you too." He nods, looking into my eyes. "We both learned some things about each other just now. I did not know your experience all those growing up years." He pauses and looks at me squarely, "Nor could you know mine."

I swallow hard, aware and grateful that a door has opened. "We'll get more chances," I say. " This conversation is just beginning. I think we've been headed here for a long time."

He hugs me close. I feel his boniness and his warmth… and the sweet stink of cigars. I smile to myself as we walk slowly back to the car.

We speak little on the drive back. The silence is comfortable. As we get to his apartment, Daddy says, "I can't tell you what this visit has meant to me." He smiles. "And I'm exhausted. I bet you are too. We'll pick up just here when you come again. I hope it's soon."

"Me too," I answer. "We've got a lot yet to learn from each other."

A hasty hug and I am off to return the car. I make the plane easily despite all of Daddy's careful warnings about the Atlanta airport. I sink into my seat and begin to gather my thoughts. The trip was not what I expected. It was richer, sadder, harder. We met as adults and juggled the needs we each had to know the truth and still to protect each other from it. I think of my own teenagers at home, and I wonder what questions they may be harboring and what I withhold in the name of protection.

II. Stories, Mostly Southern, Past and Thereafter

Lost and Found

Danny's voice pierces the country quiet of the farmhouse. "Hey, Ma, the toilet's overflowed again. There's water all over the floor," he says, but quickly adds, "some other stuff too. I'm not allowed to say the word, but you know what it is, Ma." His voice shoots up an octave. "It's gross! It's spreading! Yuck, Ma, do something!"

"You can say poop, Danny, and you can simmer down a little," Ma says in her soft Kentucky way. "You woke up Chrissy with your hollering, and now she's hollering too." It's been a long morning already for Ma, and the clock has only just gone 7:00. She stomps to the nursery off the kitchen and picks up the howling baby. Chrissy is just over a year old and does not wait well – no babies do. Ma certainly knows this, having been the oldest of eight children in a large Kentucky farm family herself. In fact she grew up in this very house. There was always somebody hollering.

She moved away for a few years. Went off to school in Louisville and then got a job writing advertising copy at the *Courier Journal*. Had a little apartment of her own, walked to work, made friends. A little taste of privacy and freedom felt great. She met and married Bill, a career Army officer. He got stationed at Fort Knox, and they moved back here, fourteen miles from the base.

As she finishes changing Chrissy, she looks longingly down the dirt road – a view she often enjoys – with its graceful live oaks and flowering crab apple trees running half a mile up to the main road. A pair of mimosas close to the house has grown tall. She recalls the year she turned twelve. Poppa made a plank seat for her up between two of the branches. He knew she wanted a break every now and then from all those younger kids. She could climb up there and hide, and they'd run all over the place looking for her. It was a great game for a few weeks until they discovered her hideout. Even when she got older she sometimes took a book up there to read where it was quiet. She wonders if the seat is still there. Maybe Danny will climb up. Some morning while Chrissy naps she might climb up there with him.

When she and Bill moved back here a few years ago, she learned to her sadness that all those beautiful trees are nourished by rambling roots that seek out water wherever it can be found. One of the best places turns out to be the old clay pipes that carry all the water to and from the house. She and Bill have made a lot of improvements since they moved out here – replaced the leaking roof on the main part of the house and added the nursery on the first floor. But all those pipes? Well, getting new pipes is way too expensive for now. Sometimes they just back up and make a mess. She's pretty sure that's the problem today. So the plumber will have to come…again.

Bill leaves for the base before dawn every day. He often compliments her, saying she knows more about running the house and land than he could ever know. As if that might make her feel better about having to do it all! Well, he's a good man, and Ma is grateful that he is at least in this country and not away in that awful war in Viet Nam. They will probably be based here permanently if the war doesn't heat up too much. Ma is glad that their kids will grow up where she did, with all that family history in their heads and bones. Maybe they'll have another child or two, but she is dead certain that she doesn't want as many as she grew up with. She sometimes wonders how her mother managed with all those kids, while Poppa tended cows and crops all day and then came home dog-tired at suppertime.

She shakes the memories away and turns back to Danny. He's making a great show, writhing and clutching his crotch. "The plumber's on his way, Danny. I already called. Just hold your horses."

"It's not my horses I'm worried about, Ma," he howls. "It's my Willie, and you always tell me I'm not *supposed* to hold on to it – at least not when anyone can see."

He groans and points to Chrissy, now placidly sucking her thumb as she sits on Ma's hip. "Well, the baby's fine," he says. "At least she's got diapers."

"Just hush your mouth, and get along now," retorts Ma. "Go on out back and do your own business in the bushes, Danny. I reckon the plumber'll be right along. Probably Mr. Mayes. He came the last time, and he was mighty prompt. Been here so many times he always puts us first."

As Danny runs off to pee, Ma walks out to the front porch with Chrissy. Looks down the road for the plumber's truck. Sets Chrissy down. She's just learning to walk, and out here she can toddle and lurch without getting into the mess inside. Maybe some bananas and cereal and she'll be set for a little while. Ma looks around. The porch sure needs work. They haven't got to the roof out here yet, and it could use some attention. It's that old corrugated metal, at least forty years old. Nobody uses that any more. There's a lot of rust, and the floor is bad too. Got some loose planks. Looks like poor white trash lives here. Heck they'll probably have to build a whole new porch by the time they can afford to do anything.

She thinks back to when her mother was alive. There were morning glories blooming all through the summer, and honeysuckle creeping over the railings. Long evenings rocking away and talking, and playing banjos and singing out here. The smell of gardenias. It seemed like life would just go on forever. She shakes her head. Well, the world has changed. Those long slow days will never come again. But every now and then, she has the sense that her mother is still right there, just out of sight. Maybe round the corner in the canning pantry, or out in back hanging clothes on the line. This place has a good grip on its history, she reckons.

She brings herself back to the here and now. Life is good. This old house will serve them for a long time. It sure beats the housing at Fort Knox where they lived for a couple of years. She's glad they moved out here. All the houses on the base look exactly alike, and she thinks the people look pretty much alike too. Lots of gossip about who does what with whom. The men all wash their cars out front every Saturday, and on Sunday the whole compound smells of smoke from the back yard barbecue grills.

It is lonely out here though. She hopes maybe somebody nice will come to buy the place just down the road. It's the only house really close by. She's noticed a "*FOR SALE*" sign on the fence down at the foot of the pasture next to the highway. She sure would like to have some company as the kids grow up. They'll need playmates. The folks that live in that place now don't like her. It's funny because she knows the wife, Mary Ann. They went to the same high school, just a grade apart. They weren't close friends, but they got along all right. At least that is the way she remembers it. But soon after she and Bill moved back here, Mary Ann told some folks at church that since Ma got married and moved back from the city, she was uppity and put on airs. And then Ma found out that Mary Ann's husband keeps a loaded gun in his truck. When she asked him about it, he said it was for protection because he carries a payroll. He told her he keeps it locked in the glove compartment all the time. But then one time Ma saw his five year old son Jim Boy sitting right there as big as life in the front seat, and playing with that gun. So she won't let Danny play there any more unless she can go along. And that's hard with the baby, and besides it isn't much fun to go where she knows she isn't wanted. One time she talked to Mary Ann about letting her boy come over to play at Danny's house. But Mary Ann told her that she'd heard there were ghosts on this old property. She said the man she'd hired to help with the chickens told her he'd caught a glimpse of his long dead cousin Roscoe passing through the henhouse. And then one evening when he was leaving, there'd been a woman dressed like a hundred years ago walking up the road in front of him. No, she said, she guessed her little Jim Boy better play at home with whatever is there, even if his stuff isn't as nice as what Danny has. She sure didn't want him around ghosts and restless souls.

Ma pushes those thoughts away. They are just ignorant, fearful folks. She looks down the road. "Look, Danny, there's the truck now," she says. But Danny isn't looking or listening. He's gone round the corner of the house to do what he needs to do. The truck comes to a stop, and the driver gets out, hefting his rusty red toolbox from the back. "Good morning, Mr. Mayes," calls Ma. "I'm sure glad to see you. It's a mess in there."

"Morning, Miz D." He shakes his head. "Can't see as how it's a good one though. Leastaways not for you, what with that toilet plugged up again. I believe that's the third time this spring that thing's stopped up on you!" He reaches in the back of the truck to retrieve a huge plunger.

"Oh yes, you're right, Mr. Mayes," she replies, looking at his tidy brown crew cut and reassuring smile. "Diapers last time and tree roots growing right into the pipes the time before."

He tells her, "Well, you know the same as me, that's the trouble with these old Kentucky farmhouses. They all got these clay pipes, miles of them wandering way out past the fence and up the road. Roots go looking for water and think the pipes are dirt."

"Guess we'll get new metal pipes one of these days," Ma says, adding, "Oh, you did a fine job last time, and we been mighty careful about the baby's diapers since then. Thought we had the problem licked. And I appreciate your coming out again today, especially so early in the morning and all. I sure hope you can fix it for a good while this time. Why look, it's even seeping out on to the porch right now."

"Well, I reckon I'll do my best," he nods reassuringly. Then he puts down the plunger and turns thoughtful. "You know, when I was just a boy, my daddy before me used to come out here. He's gone these many years now, of course. But he knew your folks, and he knew this place. Always said it had a special feel to it. Like it wouldn't surprise him if he might run into an old civil war soldier some early dawn, taking his rest under one of them oak trees. Or wounded and out of 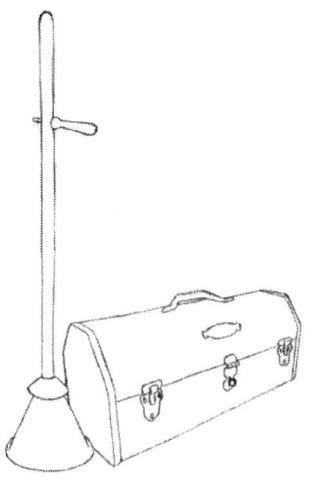 uniform, trying to make his way back home on foot without getting caught and took to prison by those outliers who hunted down deserters for the bounty. Course I didn't know what he was talking about, but it sure sounded mighty real. Kinda scared me back then. My Daddy, he said that not everyone just died and went to heaven – or the other place either. He reckoned that some souls got trapped here – maybe hadn't finished what they was sposed to get done in this life and just kept wanderin round the earth."

Just then Danny comes back. Sauntering and smiling with his big blue eyes dancing. Ma holds out his school bag. "Okay Danny, you'd better hustle. School bus'll be coming along any minute. Run along now." She looks him over and pats his backside.

"Zip up your dungarees."

"Yeah, okay, okay, Ma. Hi Mr. Mayes. What you reckon we got down there this time? A snake maybe? Not yours, I know…a real live one, I mean. Just slithering its way along through the muddy water." He grins at his own cleverness. "At least Chrissy's having a fine time. Just look at her splashing away in that puddle!" He reaches down and pats her on the head. Then he races off toward the school bus stop.

Ma shrieks. "Oh, Lordy me! She scoops up the baby and runs back into the kitchen. Fills the sink with warm water. Tries not to use too much in case it bubbles out on Mr. Mayes. Then she walks back down the hall to the bathroom. She can hear Mr. Mayes doing some powerful plunging and grunting.

"Any luck, Mr. Mayes?"

"Not so far," he answers. "There's something blocking her up, okay. Can't seem to push it through with the plunger. But it don't feel like roots this time. It's softer, and kinda big, and it moves mighty slow. I'll try my snake and then see if I can reach down there and pull it out with my hands."

Ma shudders with disgust. Considers offering to help and thinks better of it. "I'll be in the kitchen with the baby then," she calls through the door. Whatever "it" is, she doesn't want to know, and she certainly doesn't want to touch or smell it.

It is nearly an hour later when he comes into the kitchen. He has left his tools back down the hall and is holding something she has never seen before in all her life. It's about the size of a baby blanket. The texture is soft and has a rubbery flannel quality. Kind of stretchy and mostly gray with a few faded stripes and some odd shaped holes. It is slithering in his hands as if it might be alive.

"Got it," he says, smiling in triumph. "I shoulda thought of this. Haven't seen one for a right long time though. Is it yours?" He holds the slimy thing up and looks hard at her, as if to take stock, kind of measuring her for size. "No, I guess not," he says. "But then, you're kind of young yet to go losing one of these. I'm sure you still got yours. Probably always will."

"What in the world is that thing, Mr. Mayes," she says, backing away, her voice shrill, "and what was it doing in my pipes?"

"Why it's a soul, ma'am," he says. "You ain't never seen one of these? Folks lose them all the time. Why even living folks can lose a soul and never know it. Just go right on with their lives, they do. It strikes me funny that we was just talking about how my Daddy thought some of them old soldiers could still be wandering round here. The dead, may they rest in peace, don't always get to rest right away, I reckon. This house, these pipes…well, they got a lot of history." He shakes the thing and looks down again. "You got any idea whose it might be? Looks like it's been down there quite a while."

He squishes the thing into a pail. Ma just stands there, opening and closing her mouth like a goldfish. "Well," he says, "it don't seem right just to throw it out. You got a bag I can put it in? That at least shows a little more respect than this old bucket. I can check in town and see if anyone's reported a lost soul. Usually folks don't bother. Some of them don't even know it's gone missing, I guess."

He puts his jacket on to leave. "Well, anyway, your pipes are all cleared out now. They should be fine for a good long while. Just keep an eye on them diapers."

Lost As a Rabbit

My mother's sense of direction, or the lack of it, was a joke in our family. She laughed about it herself, never apologizing or seeming to feel inadequate. She knew *who* she was, even if she didn't always know *where* she was. And she was ever confident that she could find her way home.

When I was small, she'd come home from a venture into new territory and say to Herculine, our day helper, "Well, Herc, it's mighty good to be back home. For a little while there, I was just as lost as a rabbit." And they would laugh as Herc put on her sun hat to go home.

The phrase puzzled me. I was never quite sure what was particularly lost about a rabbit. But on the few occasions that I saw one or two outside in the field, I hoped they got home all right. Momma always did. She was more like Bre'er Rabbit in the Uncle Remus stories she told us than like any little rabbit lost in the woods. Clever. Sassy. Resourceful. She was always able to find her way out of a tough spot. I watched carefully so that I could learn that skill.

She made getting lost seem adventurous, rather than frightening. One of my favorite bedtime readings was the poem about James James Morrison's mother from A.A. Milne's *When We Were Very Young*. The one that begins like this:

> James, James
> Morrison Morrison
> Weatherby George Dupree
> Took great
> Care of his Mother
> Though he was only three.
> James, James
> Said to his Mother,
> "Mother," he said, said he:
> "You must never go down to the end of the town,
> If you don't go down with me."

As the story goes on, Mother slips out, goes to the end of the town, and "hasn't been heard from since." I supposed there was a tidy moral to the story. Mother got what she deserved, going out alone like that. But I was certain she would turn up soon and safe, laughing at her own foolishness. I closed the book cheerfully, hugged my mother, and thumped off to bed. Sweet dreams.

My mother was a certainty then. But as the years passed she began to get lost. Her mind became a trickster, storing odd bits of the familiar in unfamiliar places. One day I knelt on the floor next to her, trying to sort out the tangle of panty hose and shoes and underwear that seemed to have tied her legs in knots. She patted me on the head. "You're a pretty little thing," she said. "Are you my sister?"

"No, Momma," I explained. "I'm Betsy. I'm your daughter." I didn't think I needed to tell her that her sister Gracious had been dead for ten years. Not again. It was new information every time and only made her sad.

"My goodness," she replied, "how old are you?"

"I'm forty three, Momma."

She shook her head with child-like wonder, "Mercy, how old am I?"

"You're nearly eighty," I answered.

She nodded slowly, taking in this information. "You know what?" she paused, considering, " I think I've lived too long."

As weeks passed, the surroundings of her recent years grew strange. The apartment she had shared with my father since his retirement became alien territory. She was afraid. She wandered. We moved her into a nursing home. She did not complain. Her deep-set blue eyes were often blank. Even my father's particularity slipped away, although his reliability became the constant in her life. He visited her every morning. One day as I sat nearby, her eyes focused beyond me, and she smiled. "There's the North Star," she said. I turned to see my father walking toward her, carrying two large fresh strawberries.

The nursing home was called The Haven, and we counted on her moments of connection and her love of words to remind her that a haven was a safe place. We walked the halls, humming the familiar hymns of her Victorian childhood.

"Abide with me.
Fast falls the eventide.
The darkness deepens.
Lord, with me abide."

"I'm lost," she said one day, clutching my arm, her eyes filled with fear.

"Momma, you're in the Haven. You know what a haven is. It's a safe place. You're safe here." I lied the litany of reassurance.

She looked steadily at me. Unsmiling. Instructing on a matter of great importance. There was utter clarity in her china blue eyes. "You don't understand," she said, "I'm lost inside my own head...just as lost as a rabbit."

Momma's Dream

The dream was always the same. She'd just come in from school. She must have been about eight years old because she remembered her teacher was Miss Addie Black. Miss Addie was strict, but fair. Momma liked her pretty well.

Somebody called out to her as she came into the kitchen. It sounded like Aunt Laura, who had lived with the family since Poppa died two years ago. Momma didn't like her much. She was a scold. "Aura, is that you? You're late. Now you scoot right on down to the basement and fill up the coal scuttle, you hear? Keep your coat on. It's cold down there. No whining either. There is nothing to be scared of just because it's dark. And you make sure you take the time to fill that scuttle full now, or else you'll have to go back down for more. The fire's got right low and we'll be needing hot water."

She had to go; she knew it. There was no wheedling with Aunt Laura. Fear gripped her belly at the thought of those dark, uneven stairs going down into the damp of the basement. She opened the door and saw only blackness. The smell of basement surrounded her. She took the first step, and then hand over hand she felt her way down the cold stone wall. At the eighth stair, there was a sharp turn, and the dim light from upstairs was gone. She stopped and let her eyes do what adjusting they would. Listened for the scuttering of rats and mice and maybe other things. Her little cousin Alfred said the Pittibones lived down there. He couldn't tell her what it looked like, but it chased him in his nightmares. She'd hear him calling out in the night, "It's gonna get me. It's gonna get me. The Pittibones, it's gonna get me." The basement was quiet though. She moved on down the last six stairs and touched the hard earth floor.

She could just make out the coal scuttle a few feet away. There was a little light coming in around the edges of the coal chute. Something lay next to it on the floor. She looked out of the side of her eyes. She could see better in the dark if she looked sideways. She tried to make out the shape. Looked like a bunch of rags, but bigger and more solid.

She had to get the coal. No sneaking it quickly from the edges either. Aunt Laura was true to her word and would make her go back down if the scuttle was not full to the very top. She watched the pile of rags while she held her breath and counted to ten, listening for rats. Nothing. She stepped one foot forward and brought the other one up to it. Step. Slide. Step. Slide. And then she saw the face in the rags.

It was Poppa. Lying on the floor, his head against the furnace. Not moving. Just lying there with his eyes wide open.

The dream always stopped there, and she woke up.

The nightmare had never varied. Not in forty years. It came less often as she got older, but it still came. Then when Momma was well into her fifties, her older sister Gracious came to live and die with Momma and our family. The dream returned with its old vividness. She was there again, the eight-year-old Aura edging down the dark stairs. Staring into Poppa's white, bloated, blank eyed face.

This time the dream did not end as usual. As she stood frozen in terror next to what was Poppa, she heard a voice calling from above the stairs, from the light of the house. But the voice was different. It wasn't Aunt Laura scolding. This voice sounded like her big sister Gracious. "Get up, Hant," the voice commanded. "You're scaring my baby sister."

As she watched, the figure in the rags rose. It took quite a time for Poppa to stand all the way up to his full six feet, three inches. He was dressed in his Sunday clothes. He reached down and picked up his hat from the rags and put it on his head. He was completely restored and smiling his customary funny half smile. He bowed at the waist and tipped his hat. "I'm terribly sorry," he said. "I had no idea." And he walked past the little girl and up the stairs. Momma never dreamed the dream again.

Worth Troubling Over

The six of us had just finished a light supper. My attempt for simple, but elegant had been successful. It usually goes well. We know the drill, and over the years, we have been blessed with a number of musical friends who enjoy talking and playing together. Tonight three of them who play violin, viola and cello would join my husband Frank at the piano to play a Mozart quartet. There is something very beautiful and somehow civilized in both playing and hearing this music from the 18th century, live and in a small space, as the composer intended. It would be a wonderful evening.

I heard Frank strike an A on the piano, and the strings began to tune up. I snuffed the candles and began to stack the plates. I would join them as soon as the table was cleared. That would take only a few minutes.

But when I walked into the kitchen, I found our other guest already there, dish towel in hand. Now, my mother's daughter has clear guidelines for courtesy and hospitality. In my careful Southern upbringing, there was little place for guests on the clean up crew. And no place at all for this kindly older gentleman. If I had remembered that he was not playing this evening, I would have hustled him out of the dining room with all the others.

So, I smiled warmly and said, "Oh how kind of you, Dr. Stanbury, but you really don't need to help. Please join the others in the living room. I'll be with you shortly."

He looked down at our large black Labrador, Firmly Jones, who was taking up much of the floor space between door and sink. "Well," he said, "it doesn't look like that dawg is going to help you much. And they certainly don't need or want me to help them tune up. I'm off the stage tonight, and I'd be honored to keep you company. We can square this kitchen away in no time."

Graciousness trumped my mother's rules. It would be rude to say no. "Why, thank you," I said, as I lured Firmly Jones away with a scrap of food. I reached for the gate, pretty sure that he would not be welcome in the living room either. Dogs tend to howl at string sounds.

Making conversation, Dr. Stanbury said, "I know Frank is from New York. But you don't sound like an Easterner. Where do you come from?"

I chuckled and said, "Well, from the sound of "dawg", not very far from where you come from!"

He cocked his head. "And where would that be?"

I identified myself in the way that Southerners have done for many generations. We don't just name the town, but also claim the family lineage. "Well, I was born in Charlotte, but my mother's family all came from Durham. She was a Holton."

He looked puzzled and was quiet for a few seconds. "Not Aura Holton, who taught English at Durham High School?"

"Why yes," I said, "my mother did teach at the high school. I think she was there for about five or six years. Look, here she is."

Among the pictures on our kitchen wall is one of my mother as a young woman about twenty three or twenty four years old, taken years before I was born. Her long dark hair is pulled back and she has a wide smile. I took it down and passed it to him.

His face softened. I thought I saw tears. "Yes, that's Aura Holton," he said. He was quiet for a minute, studying the photograph. Then he looked at me and said, "Your mother was one of the most important people in my adolescent life. She thought I was worth troubling over. She thought I might amount to something."

He told me that he had been back to Durham a number of times and had tried without success to find her or any member of the Holton family. "I wanted to see her, to thank her and show her I did come out all right after all. I even went over to the high school and looked through the records," he said. "She was in there in the history, and so was her brother Quinton. He was principal for a time. I remember some of the boys pouring a bucket of water out of the second story window onto his head one day as he was leaving. He recognized them and made them clean the bathrooms for weeks after that." He smiled at the memory. "But I never could find any address for her, or any of the family. There's a Baptist Church now on Watts Street where their house used to be." We were both quiet for what felt like a very long minute.

"Is she gone?" he asked gently.

"Yes," I said, "almost 10 years ago."

I asked him to tell me about her - this young woman who became my mother.

He looked way back in time. "She was small," he said, "not as big as a minute. We were big rawboned boys in a poor mill town. It was her job to teach us Shakespeare, and she knew we'd never sit still to read it, even if we could. So she read to us. She was a tiny little bit of a woman, sitting on her desk so she'd be tall enough to see us all and make sure we paid attention. She made Hamlet come alive... and then die. She taught us scrappy tough kids that people were not always what they seemed to be. Even kings like Lear and Macbeth were fooled by folks they thought were on their side. We all had experience with bullies, and we knew about trickery. We got that one."

He went on, "But you know the very best thing she did? She went down and asked the foreman at the lumber mill to give us some scrap wood so we could build a model stage. And he did! Most of us had lived around mills all our lives. Lumber, cigarettes, cotton…we knew about mills all right. She made us study the dimensions of that old Globe stage and do the math to shrink it down to build a model that we were proud to show off."

He went on to say that while he had been in her class for only one year, she kept an eye on him until he graduated and was launched onto the next steps of his education. We agreed that having Aura Holton's eye on you could be daunting as well as comforting.

We had missed the first round of Mozart by the time we left the kitchen to join the musicians. We took Momma's photo by way of explanation and asked them to play a second time. They played, and the music was indeed sublime. It was yet another visit to another time.

The gifts of that evening have remained precious. Our guest gave me a sense of my mother before I knew her. He gave her a touch of immortality. I gave him back a moment in time. A moment when he was a youngster facing the world ahead and forging a life shaping relationship with a teacher who believed he was worth troubling over.

The Picture Show

We stood in front of the candy counter, my brother Jerry and I. He was fourteen, and I was not quite eleven. "Hurry up, will you?" he ordered. "Here, take those." He pointed to a pack of Necco wafers. "The movie's about to start, and Kenny and Grant are saving us seats. Hurry up!"

I watched the lights chase each other around the candy case. Milk Duds, Good N Plenty, Jujubes, Goobers... Finally, I pointed to a Hershey bar with almonds, and the pimply-faced boy behind the counter pushed it over the top.

"C'mon," said Jerry, moving toward the door. The lights were going down as we made our way into the theater. I stopped, unable to focus in the dark. "*Hurry up!*" Jerry hissed. "They'll be way down front." He moved ahead. I began to make out heads and seats in the darkness, and I followed.

This was only the second movie I'd been to in my whole life. Movies were expensive, and we did not go often. My first movie was *Snow White* with Momma last year on my birthday. Jerry had not wanted to bring me today. He and Momma had a big argument about it, and I begged and cried, and Jerry said I was a baby and he wasn't taking a baby to the movie with his friends. No way. So I held my breath and stopped crying. Momma said she'd pay the way for both of us if he took me. That meant Jerry wouldn't have to spend his allowance, so he finally said okay.

Once we left home, he didn't have to be nice to me though. He just had to let me follow him. And that was embarrassing enough. "You can tag along, but don't talk to my friends. Don't you dare say a word," he warned.

The theater went totally dark, except for the jumping lights from the Bugs Bunny cartoon and the red EXIT lights that marked the curtained doors on either side of the screen. I tripped on my shoelace. I didn't fall, but several people looked around, annoyed. Jerry looked over his shoulder, but didn't say a word. "He'll never bring me again, no matter what Momma says," I thought.

Grant and Kenny were on the fourth row at the far left side. There was one seat next to Kenny and another one three rows behind, almost in the corner, with Grant's baseball jacket on it. "Guess they couldn't save four together," Jerry whispered, "you slide in over there."

I was pretty sure they could have saved another seat. They just didn't want to sit with me. Kenny was sneaky like that. He and Jerry probably planned it. Grant wouldn't have set that up. He was always nice to me. Looked out for me when we played outside, and let me play in left field when the boys played baseball. I was the only girl.

I climbed over seven people to the next to last seat. I couldn't see very well from the corner. But at least I was there. I'd made it to the movies. I put Grant's jacket on the floor and then picked it up because the floor felt sticky under my feet, and I didn't want Grant to get mad at me. I knew he loved that jacket.

"Here, I'll hold it for you." The man sitting next to me in the corner took the coat and unwadded it. He spread it out on his lap.

"Thanks," I said. I loosened my grip on the Hershey bar and opened the end of the wrapper. The chocolate had partly melted and was soft and sticky on my hands. I licked my fingers, careful not to get my skirt dirty. The cartoon ended with a flash of Porky Pig saying, "That's all, folks!"

"Here," said the man, "here's a handkerchief." He took my hand and began to wipe my fingers one by one. "Aren't you kind of little to be here all by yourself?" he whispered.

"Oh, my big brother's here with me. See, he's right down there with his friends, Kenny and Grant," I answered, pulling my hand loose and pointing to the fourth row, where there were now three empty seats. They had ditched me.

I started to cry. The movie was beginning and the theater was dark again. The man held out a pack of Neccos. He pulled one out and pressed it against my hand. "Here you go, have one," he whispered. "There's a whole pack." He left his hand on my skirt.

I was scared. What if they didn't come back soon? What if they didn't come back at all? How would I get home? I didn't want the man to see that I was crying. I stood up. They must be down there. They couldn't have left me. "Sit down," he said, pulling gently on my arm. "They'll be back by the end. Just sit down like a good girl now and watch the movie." He pushed the pack of Neccos in my hand and curled my fingers around it. His hand was damp and warm and he wouldn't let go of mine. His other arm now rested on the back of my seat. It was near the top, but I knew it had not been there just a second ago. I leaned forward. Then I half rose.

"Hey, where are you going?" he asked softly. "I have your jacket." He patted his lap. "Don't leave without it. Your brother will be mad." I knew the man was right. Jerry would be mad and so would

Grant. They'd never bring me anywhere again. I stood there, stone still, and then sat back down. The man squeezed my hand. The person sitting behind us said, "Shh."

I didn't know what was happening, but I knew that something was very wrong. Terror won. I fled, climbing over seven angry folks again, and leaving Grant's baseball jacket behind. The man just sat very still.

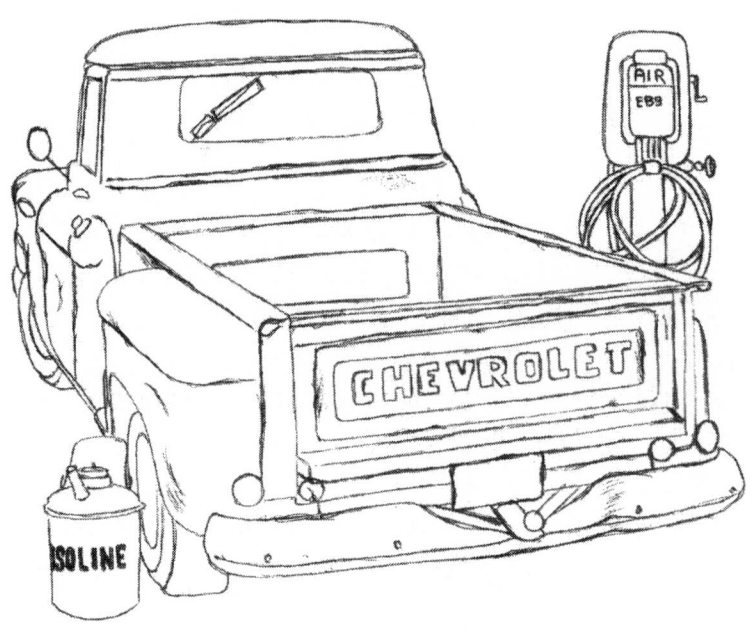

The Gas Can

George was going to be late. That's all there was to it. He was never late anywhere. He allowed for traffic; he allowed for weather; he allowed for a slow down when the school bus stopped, scattering small children into the road like marbles. But life had outmaneuvered him this morning. His wife Yamila and their baby Franklin had both been sick in the night and were no better this morning. Fevers and coughs had pushed the seconds at home closer together, and now he was stuck in rush hour traffic. The last quarter mile had taken ten minutes.

He'd be fined for every minute after 8:00 that his cart at the shopping mall was not open for business. The contract was clear. Management wanted the place cheerful, busy, and ready to ring-a-ching-ching merrily for sixteen hours out of twenty-four as the Christmas shoppers brought in a year's profit. Lakeside Mall was upscale, permitting only "internationally interesting" carts. He and Yamila had stocked their cart with hand carved wooden puzzle boxes from her native Costa Rica. They had Christmas angels and stars, as well as turtles and whales and even an alligator. No other cart had anything like theirs, and sales had been good. Lakeside was a plum place to be, and there was no negotiating about the rules: Three fines for lateness and you were out. Never mind a sick wife and baby. He saw his profit for the day melting away.

He turned on the radio for the traffic report. No hope for miles. His gas gauge looked ominous too. And it was as unforgiving as the mall management. Low was low, and empty was empty. He began to squeeze across the six-lane freeway toward the exit ramp. Horns blared and fingers flew, but the '98 Dodge made it off, and coughed to a standstill just before the ramp.

There was mercy though. Looking up at the exit, he spied a Gulf sign. He had no gas can, but surely the station would have one on hand. He trudged up the ramp with hope in his heart. It was just possible he might still make it on time.

But hope was quickly dashed. The station had no gas cans. Yes, they used to keep a couple around for this kind of emergency, the mechanic explained, but the last one had ridden off with an ungrateful driver a while back. Guessed he wouldn't supply them any more. "You just can't trust folks. Everybody is out for himself," he said. The guy was warming up for a sermon on ingratitude, and George turned to leave. He had troubles enough, and no help in sight.

Or was there? He saw a pick up truck at the air pump. The engine was running, but there was no one in the cab. The lettering on the door said "Joe's Roofing." There was no address, no phone number, no contractor's number, no more information at all. George shook his head. He knew all too well that the only reason a guy would leave his engine running like that is that he knows from experience that it won't start again if he shuts it off. And the reason there is no contact information on the truck is that "Joe's" only office is inside that small cab and he'll be gone as soon as he makes enough money for a few days' booze.

BUT, in the back of the truck there was a gas can. George studied it. He couldn't just take the can. It belonged to Joe. So he waited. And sure enough, out of the men's room came a figure that had to be Joe.

He was a scary looking guy. Big. Black. Wide scar running all the way down the left side of his face. Front tooth missing. Dirty torn jeans. "Do rag" mostly covering his head. George would have crossed the street to avoid him at night.

BUT there was a gas can in his truck.

George took a deep breath and walked toward the guy who must be Joe. "Hey man," he said. "I'm out of gas down there on the freeway. Right at the exit. Would you sell me your gas can? Maybe ten bucks?" Joe scowled. "Fifteen? Look, I'm desperate…gotta get to work, gonna lose my job, got a sick wife and baby. Could you maybe even lend me the can for a few minutes? I can bring it right back. I'm on the edge of the ramp pointing right this direction. Five minutes for twenty bucks. How bout it?"

Not a word. Another expensive minute ticked by while Joe looked over George's clean cut white Caucasian self from top to bottom.

He reached a decision. "Man," he said, "You can *have* my gas can. I been where you are. You in tough shape." He swung the can out of the truck and handed it over. George reached into his pocket to find some cash. Joe waved him away. "Just take it, and good luck to you, man. Looks like you need it."

George said his hasty thanks, took the can, filled it, and ran back down the ramp. He had managed to leave the car right at the edge of the ramp, so he was able to swing back on. He got to the mall fifteen minutes late, which translated into a fine of $45. Then sales boomed, and the profits for the day turned out to be the best so far this season.

As he drove home at midnight on his full tank of gas, he thought about Joe. His day had been set right by Joe's kindness. Joe was an itinerant black roofer in the Deep South. He was doing the best he could with what he had, but he didn't have much.

George wondered what would have happened if their roles had been reversed. Would a poor black down and outer have approached the buttoned down George for help? And if George had seen this scary black guy coming toward him, would he have stayed to find out why?

He didn't think so. It wasn't a good feeling.

When he got home, the baby was sleeping. The fever was gone, and his wife woke enough to say she felt better too. Still wide-awake, he told her about his day. They were both relieved that sales had been good. And they gave considerable thought to the scary looking roofer Joe, and said a prayer for him. Many years later, that gas can still sits by their fireplace as a reminder that kindness has no color.

Look Again

It was a scene that I knew from memory. I saw myself in the young mother walking with me. Long blonde hair tied back, jeans and sturdy boots, carrying a six week old infant in a sling while holding the hand of his three-year old brother, and calling ahead to tell a fast moving five-year old to slow down. All boys. I smiled to myself. It really could have been me, years ago with the same constellation of young sons and a similar delight in being out of doors with them.

That time has passed, and now I am the grandmother, not the mother. The mother in this scene is Rebecca, and she is married to Andrew, the youngest of our three sons. Their sons are baby Micah, three-year old Eli, and Samuel, who is five. The setting is the northwest coast of the state of Washington, not the familiar mountains of western North Carolina or the Berkshires in Massachusetts. I am looking through older eyes as I walk with these boys. I recall childhood walks on Greybeard Mountain with my mother and father and later ones with our own children in the Berkshires.

Rebecca and I walked into a fairy tale day with these boys. Tall trees going up as far as we could see. Sunlight slipping through them, shafting to form patches on the ground. There was no sound, except for the occasional birdcall and answer. Walking down the gradual grade of the trail, we would reach the shallow water of the bay in less than a mile. Completing our little group was Abigail, a large and gentle old black German shepherd. There were no other cars at the trailhead. We would have the place to ourselves.

"Should we lock the car?" I asked. "Then we could leave our stuff inside."

"Oh yes," Rebecca replied. "We'll need our hands free to hold theirs, and to carry the treasures they are sure to find. Oh, and I've got some little boxes of raisins in my backpack. Food always comes in handy, and raisins give quick energy. The boys like them."

A few hundred yards down the trail, we saw a man coming toward us, wearing several layers of clothing, and pushing a cart. It was not a grocery cart, but an old wooden one with sturdy wheels. The kind sometimes used to move gardening debris. This one contained a tarp and some clothing and backpack stuff. It looked right at home in the forest. The man was small and wizened, with red cheeks and gnarled hands. He tipped his cap and nodded as he passed.

"He looks like the woodcutter in a fairy tale," I said quietly. "But I bet he's not."

"No," Rebecca answered. "This is the last stop on the train line before the Canadian border. Homeless folks pretty much get off here. They'll get picked up if they try to cross over the border without the necessary papers. There are a good many shelters in town, and this climate is not too harsh—lots of rain, but usually not freezing cold. He's a short little guy. I bet he could probably even curl up and sleep on the tarp in that cart. I wonder if he has any food. I wish I'd thought to offer him a box of raisins."

We came out of the forest a few minutes later. The sun made rainbows on the water as the children collected small stones and waded. Micah mercifully slept on. Sam started to climb a tree and thought better of it when the trunk proved slippery. We sat on a big rock in the sun, watching hawks soar over our heads.

Rebecca was a long distance hiker. She and Andrew had met each other a few hundred miles up the Appalachian Trail and walked the remaining two thousand miles together. They knew each other well by the time they married a year later.

"Did your parents take you hiking when you were growing up?" I asked.

"Not much," she replied, "but they were very outdoorsy people. We lived way out in the country. My dad hunted and brought in all our meat. I don't recall ever buying meat at the grocery. Mom grew most of our vegetables, and I learned a lot about gardening. Andy says we eat well from her lessons, especially out here with the long growing season. When I was a kid, mom canned a lot of our harvest. But now, I mostly freeze things. It's easier and tastes better."

"Sounds like a wholesome way to grow up, "I said.

"We just thought it was the way the world was for everybody," she replied. "But we did do something else that we knew was special just to us."

I raised my eyebrows to question. It was fun getting to know her this way.

"As my sister Katie and I got older, Mom took in puppies that had been selected for training as Seeing Eye dogs. They could begin training when they were a year old, and our job was to help care for them during that first year and teach them gentleness and obedience. Things like coming when called, sitting and lying down on command, and picking up a ball of wool and bringing it back without damaging it. That part was to train for a gentle mouth. We got to pick out one puppy at a time and raise it for a year before taking it back to the Seeing Eye trainers. Then we got to pick out another one that very day and bring it home and start all over again. We did it for a long time."

"Wasn't it hard to give them up?" I asked.

"No," she said. "That was part of the contract we made, and we understood it from the very first day. We had a job to do, and these were the rules. We were to care for the puppy for a year, feed and train it, give it back and bring another one home. I learned from my mom that if children are given clear expectations, they manage some tough things pretty easily. I hope I can do as well by these boys," she smiled. "What about you? I'll bet your life growing up in the deep South a generation ago had its own rules!"

I laughed. "It sure did. We were taught the usual Southern rules about manners and politeness. We learned those lessons well. Saying 'Yes Ma'am' and 'Please' and 'Thank you very much.' And we absorbed some of the unwritten rules about race and gender. Some deep and awful, and some that just seemed silly…like white girls not being allowed to go barefoot. There were also some clear distinctions about what boys could do and how girls had to behave."

Becky smiled. "Not so much for us. We had no brothers to do the heavy lifting! My Dad cut the firewood and made sure that Katie and I learned to stack it just right. We spent most Saturdays that way. We didn't like it, but we did it. That was the way he'd been brought up, and he was very strict. We were expected to toe the mark, and we did."

We were quiet for a minute, looking at the water and the children.

"Were both your parents Southern?" she asked.

"Oh, no," I answered. "Momma met my Dad when he came to the South from the Midwest to work his way through school. He thought he'd be a minister, but ended up studying psychology and education at Duke instead. He'd grown up hard. His parents were itinerant musicians. That's probably where Andrew gets the music gene!"

"Does Andy know about this?" Rebecca asked. "He's never mentioned this piece of his family, but he's never met a stringed instrument he couldn't pick up and play either."

"His uncle Jerry is the same way," I answered. "But I guess Daddy never talked to the grandchildren about his growing up. He was happy to put it behind him. I'll tell you what I know if you like."

"Oh yes, please," said Rebecca. And so I told her what I could remember of the life that formed my Daddy.

The family had traveled the Chautauqua circuit from New York State through the Middle West every year from early spring through summer. Granddad was a violinist who served as concertmaster of the orchestra. Grandma played piano and any other keyboard she could find. When the fall came and the season ended, he would use their summer earnings to buy a "fix it up" house wherever they landed. When spring came and the music began, they'd sell that house for a profit and head out again. They camped all summer.

In addition to fiddling, Granddad was a fine carpenter. He made all the improvements he could while the family lived in the winter house. He earned money doing odd jobs for other folks too, and if the town had a movie theater, he'd pick up extra cash by playing the organ while people were finding their seats. It was before the "talkies," and many theaters had organs as part of the entertainment. Grandma could usually find a position playing piano and directing a church choir for the winter. She took in sewing and mending too. She was good at it, but doing it made her peevish. Daddy went to a different school each year and did odd jobs to add to the family income. The winter he was ten, he worked for a printer, picking up type from the floor. Then he'd sweep up and close the shop. He could always find work delivering groceries and eggs.

"That's about it, I guess. It taught my daddy a lot of things, good and bad."

"Well, I guess so! I wish I'd known him," said Rebecca. "And I thought my parents were as self sufficient and close to the earth as anyone ought to be!" She smiled protectively at Baby Micah, just beginning to stir in his sling. Down at the shoreline Sam and Eli were improvising a raft. "The water is too cold to tempt them," she said, "but we should probably be closer."

She waved to the boys as we started down to the water. "I wonder what memories are being stored up in those little blonde heads," she said. "I hope they remember the good stuff."

"Daddy told us a lot about the good stuff: how he learned to make a campfire and find his way by landmarks and keep warm and dry in bad weather. But there were hard things too, and he made sense of them in odd ways. I mostly just kept quiet when he went off on a tangent."

"Tell me one," said Rebecca.

"Well, everyone was living hand to mouth, and so there was a lot of stealing. He learned early to put things away if they had a place, or to hide them if they didn't. But things got stolen anyway...warm socks, a pocketknife that slipped out. His parents never scolded when that happened. His father's rule was that if you left something out and someone stole it, he probably needed it more than you did. You should not wish him ill, but count your blessings and be grateful for all you have."

"Well, I'm sure not teaching our kids that," said Rebecca. "Stealing is just wrong no matter how you look at it."

I nodded. "Right you are," I said. " I never understood Daddy's take on that. My parents took me to Sunday school every week and to Bible School in the summer. I memorized all the books of the Bible and the Ten Commandments. I knew the Bible taught, 'Thou shalt not steal.' It all seemed pretty clear to me, but the only times I tried to reason with Daddy about stealing, he just looked sad and shook his head and said that nobody wanted to steal. Some folks just had to. Something in how sad he was kept me from going on about it. But I sure taught our kids not to take anything that wasn't theirs."

Rebecca shook her head and smiled. " Funny, how there can be baggage even in things that look so clear. Andy and I are bringing up little ones now, and we haven't had to face the honesty question yet. We're just at the 'Don't touch his juice' stage, and even that gets pretty loud sometimes."

Sam and Eli came up from the water's edge, clearly played out and in search of food. She gave each boy a small box of raisins and a swig of water before we began the walk back. They revived quickly, scampering ahead. When we came to a fork in the path, they stopped. Sam and I took the high road to the right while Rebecca and Eli and the now awake Micah took the low road. We all got back to the car at the same time and laughed as we met. It had been a great morning.

Somehow the car was unlocked. We helped the boys back into their seats, fastening their belts, and got into the car. I reached for my bag on the floor of the front seat and noticed it was open. "Odd," I thought. "I'm sure I zipped it up." Reaching in, I found that my wallet had no money. Not a single bill. Nothing else was disturbed. My credit cards and driver's license were still right there. But all the money was gone.

Rebecca looked worried. "I'm sure I pushed the lock button on my keys, but maybe it didn't catch. The battery connection's been funny. How much was it?"

"About a hundred dollars," I said. She frowned and pressed the lock button on her keys. No click. No beep. The battery was dead. My cash had doubtless gone with the tramp in the forest. There was no one else around.

I tried to reassure Rebecca, reflecting back on Daddy's credo. "Funny, isn't it? We were just talking about what my Daddy believed. Why I can almost hear him speak. Remember? 'If someone steals from you, his need was probably greater than yours. Bear him no ill will, and consider your own good fortune.' Well, I've sure got plenty of good fortune right here with you!"

It sounded good, but it went hollow pretty fast. Never mind his need. I thought of him rummaging through my bag with his dirty hands. I wondered what he really had under that tarp on his cart. He no longer looked like a charming woodcutter. He was a tramp…probably a drunk. And he stole my things. I was outraged.

After a while I had a new thought. The wallet was still there after all, and my identification and credit cards. I would not have to report them lost. And the drivers license too. I would not have to call the airline to report that I had no ID, file for identify theft, or go to the police station and make a crime report in order to fly home. I was out a hundred dollars. That was it. I turned to Rebecca. "Well, from the looks of that man, he certainly needed the cash more than I do." I thought again of Daddy. Maybe I'd have to look at this stealing issue again.

We drove on. I thought some more. The easiest course for the robber would have been to grab my bag and move right along. He might have taken out the cash and thrown the wallet in the undergrowth down the road. I'd never have found it. Or he might have kept the credit cards and traded them for something else he needed. But he took the risk of standing for several minutes at our car, clearly not belonging there. One look would tell anybody that. He lifted out my money and took time to put the wallet back in my bag. What if we had returned? What if another car had pulled into the trailhead? It was even possible that a park ranger might have come along. He could not have run away quickly, not with that cart, which surely carried all he owned.

But even a thief has his standards. And one of his must have been to take only what he needed. Years after the conversation with my father, I could begin to see his teaching from a new perspective. The tramp needed the money far more than I did, and he wronged me as little as possible in the taking of it. A few months later, I find that indeed I bear him no ill will. I even have a grudging respect for his standards.

If Hans Christian Andersen had written this story, the man would have returned my money and been transformed into a king for doing the right thing. Since it is my story, I wish him well. I am grateful for what the experience taught me. My life view is expanded by the event, the conversation with Rebecca, the memory of my father's strong conviction, and the opportunity to look at it again.

Following this experience, I began to carry a few dollars in my pocket whenever I go downtown. When I run into beggars on the streets of Boston, I say hello, maybe have a brief conversation, and give the dollars away one by one. The surprising thing to me is how little it costs me. The conversations are perhaps as important as the dollars. Daddy would be glad.

III. Essays

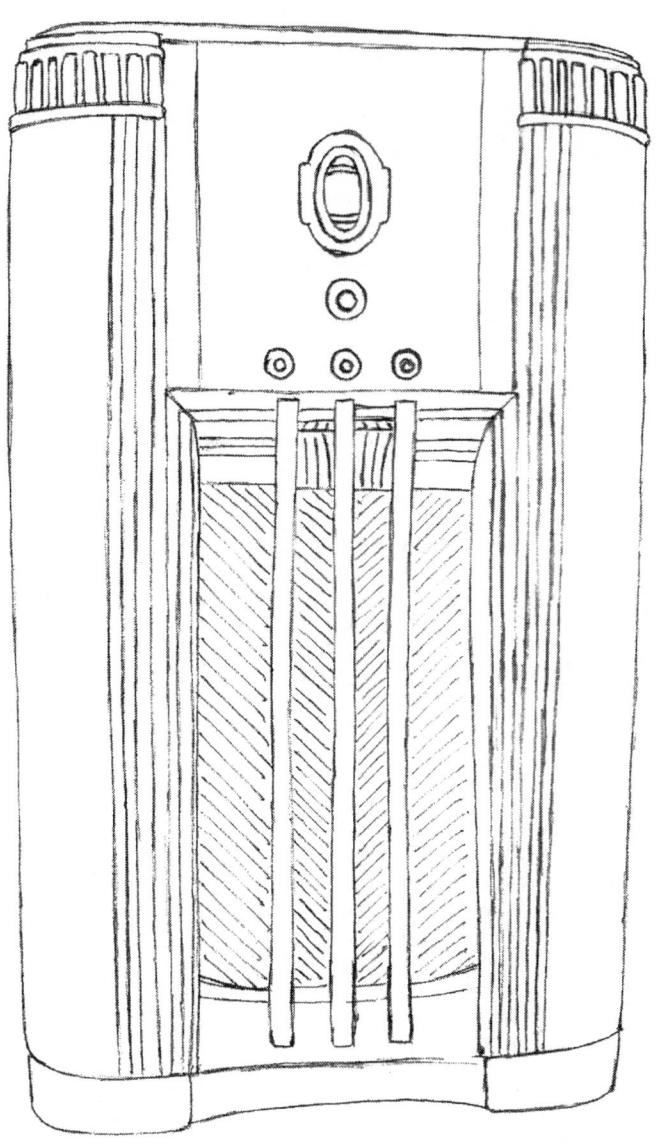

Suddenly, I Remember

Last week the young gum-chewing girl in the movie theater ticket booth charged me senior rates without even asking. I realize that this isn't sudden. It's been coming a long time.

I first noticed it some years ago as I watched the Oliver Stone film *Nixon* with my sons, three well informed, state of the art young adults. As white male followed white male across the screen of shame, one or another would ask, "Who was he?" I'll grant that one looked pretty much like the next, and the levels of mediocrity were similar. They'd heard of G. Gordon Liddy, but John Dean, Jeb Stuart Magruder, and Alexander Haig were faceless and nameless to these youngsters. The events that I had watched with amazement that became disgust were, to them, history.

Looking at family scrapbooks a few days later, one son called to his brother, "Hey, George, come look at this! Look at Momma. Isn't she adorable? She looks so fifties."

I mustered all my dignity. "Excuse me, that's no costume. I was the fifties." They laughed and I laughed too. But it gave me pause. Suddenly I'm history. I remember.....

I remember the first time I sensed that the grown ups in charge of the world felt unsafe themselves. December 7, 1941. My family sat around the radio. It was a floor model, taller than me, with a yellow light in its middle. The cloth webbing over the sound box was divided into arches just like the stained glass windows in church. We heard over and over, "The Japanese have bombed Pearl Harbor." Later, there was a voice so strange to my southern ears that I barely took in the words. They made no sense to me anyway. "A day that will live in infamy." Where was infamy? And how could a day live there? I didn't ask these questions because the grown ups looked so serious that I was afraid. Momma said that the owner of the funny voice was the greatest man alive, and Daddy countered that not everyone thought so. That voice belonged to Franklin Delano Roosevelt, and it would become very familiar in the months that followed. I didn't understand what had happened to the world, but I could tell that my parents were mad and scared. So, I was scared too.

On Christmas my Aunt Gracious came from Chicago to visit us. I wondered where Chicago was. Maybe it was near Pearl Harbor. I asked and was embarrassed when everyone laughed and no one answered. I remember the flag draped coffins in the cold train station. There were rows and rows of them, on flatbeds with wheels. I wanted to touch them, but I was afraid. Daddy said they had brave dead soldiers in them. I wondered how he knew they were brave. I wondered if he was sure they were dead. What if someone made a mistake? What if a live one was in there? What if a dead one knocked? What was "dead" anyway? Was there blood in those boxes? Was it red and runny or was it dried brown and scabby like skinned knees? I looked under the flatbeds to see if there were drips but there weren't. Daddy asked me what I was looking for, and I said, "Oh, nothing." Maybe the boxes only had bones with folded up uniforms and a flag beside them. I was afraid to ask my questions, so I just imagined, and wished that the station weren't so cold and that my aunt would come. She always smelled of lavender, and Momma used our ration coupons to buy butter when she came. I liked butter.

We had green shades at every window for black out drills, and each of us was responsible for a room when the siren went off. I got the living room, where everyone came to wait until the all clear sounded. I was glad I didn't have to run through the dark house all by myself. We kept those shades for years after the war ended. Momma pulled them most of the way down when we had the measles, so our eyes wouldn't get weak. Children don't get measles any more, or polio.

I remember polio. All the playgrounds and pools were closed because of contagion. We went to church though. I wondered why church was okay because there were lots of people there too. Had God purified the building? Then I decided God had failed because I got polio anyway. In spite of all the offerings and hymns, the prayers and preaching, and even memorizing all of the books of the Bible, I got polio and had to wear braces and horrible shoes for ages. It was the beginning of my uncertainty about God.

During the long, hot, shade down summers, most of our world existed under the dining room table. Momma helped us map out the Hundred Acre Wood on the worn carpet under the table, and she made stuffed piglets and rabbits and a Tigger and an Owl and an Eeyore out of scraps of fabric. The carpet was once a deep red but it had faded and spotted until Momma said it looked like the floor of a forest. She didn't let us take food under the table, but sometimes we sneaked it there anyway, and called the dog to eat up the evidence.

I was usually Pooh, the silly old Bear, and my older brother Jerry was the resourceful Christopher Robin, who directed the stories and got Pooh out of scrapes. Sometimes Jerry would get bored with the game and wander off, leaving me in the pit of the Horrible, Harrible Heffalump, or stuck in Piglet's house until I howled for him to come back. Momma said I could get out all by myself, but I knew that the story didn't go that way.

I remember the day the war ended. We children had been sent out for a penny walk. I don't think children go for penny walks any more. My older sister Meg was twelve, and she was in charge. She was always in charge of everything. My brother and I took turns flipping the penny at each corner. Tails, we turned left; heads, right. It was routine for keeping us occupied on long afternoons, especially when the broadcast of the Metropolitan opera was on. It looked like chance the way the coin flipped. So I used to wonder why we always ended back at home on time. Why didn't we ever flip ourselves too far away to ever get back? I suspected my brother or sister of cheating but I couldn't figure out how they did it.

Anyway, that day we were almost home, just turning right on heads with only a block to go if the flips went right. I could see our house. All of a sudden the church bells started to ring. I heard a wailing sound. High pitched. Scary. I looked over toward the sound and saw Herculine, our day helper, sitting on the front porch. She had thrown her apron over her head and was howling. A solid lump of noise right there at our house! Momma ran up the street toward us and caught us up with hugs and tears, saying over and over, "The war is ended, the war is ended." I didn't understand and I was scared because Momma was crying. I'd never seen Momma cry.

All of this happened over half a century ago. We're at war again. Polio is gone. And measles, only to be followed by a host of emerging and terrifying illnesses. I don't feel like I'm history most of the time, but I am considerably shorter and more wrinkled. And when I'm tired, my left leg drags.

How I See It - The View From 184

To begin with, I realized just a few days ago that THEY have been here over half my life. I am nearly eighty years old, having been built in 1935. The previous people were quite different. They were quieter, but the man drank. And neater, though the woman really did sweep things under the rug. No one ever knew.

And they liked the dark. I wore heavy drapes then, with scrim filler curtains in the middle. To keep out the sunlight or to keep a blank face to the outside? I was never sure which. There was a mirror facing the kitchen sink. I didn't know if it was for last minute primping or to see if someone came up from behind. The door was always locked when they left the house or went to bed. They were vigilant. My windows and gutters were cleaned every year. I presented a sparkling face. I did get a little water in the basement every now and then, but mostly I felt safe.

The yard was perfect. They got the leaves up almost as they fell. The yews by the door were perfectly trimmed into round ball shapes like ice cream cones. No spike ever strayed out of line. The flower garden was symmetrical in shades of pink and white. I'm painted white too, so we looked good together.

THEY, the new people, came over 40 years ago. There were four of them at first, two big and two small. They spoke of liking me, but then they pulled down all my drapes. She took down the mirror in the kitchen. Said she certainly didn't want to watch herself at the sink. He wanted room for a large piano, so even before they moved in, he hired carpenters to attack my walls. My cozy little room at the end of the living room was hacked away and merged right into the larger space. The living room was long and thin and huge – the proportions all wrong. They moved the bathroom and the hall coat closet and made them smaller. I missed the closet. It was oversized and private and had a window; it was the only place in the house where I could look out on the pond and the woods. And then there was the once perfect yard. Leaves fell as they always had, but when THEY came, the leaves piled up. The small people made great heaps of them and hid and jumped and yelled. Eventually THEY would come out and rake everything into a tarp and haul it off to the woods. Good for land fill, they said, and much less expensive than having someone bag them up in plastic bags.

And the yews, which had flanked the front steps for over 35 years? At first THEY neglected them for long periods while they sprouted odd branches and lost their perfect roundness. Then they cut them into tidy, ridiculous shapes; the children would guess what they were and laugh. It was embarrassing. And after a while they tired of this and simply pulled them out. The evergreen guardians were replaced by a helter skelter garden of multi colored flowers and herbs. There were a few years when they even grew tomatoes in the front garden. She said it got the only full sun on the property. I thought it not classy at all and was relieved when they gave that up.

When the third small person came along, they attacked my walls again. This time they tore out the entire back wall and the stairs. I grew a whole room bigger. Lots of windows and light. The outside almost moved inside. At first I felt exposed and unsafe, but I learned to love the warmth and brightness. I was almost part of the woods and pond.

I began to like the new people despite their noise and untidiness. There were lots of extra people in and out. A couple of big dogs moved in. The small people sometimes fought with each other, but they always loved the dogs. Even slept with them. HE worked a lot, and he made great sounds on the piano when he was home. SHE went out to work when the little people were at school, but I think I was the only one that knew she was gone. Unlike the first people, she did not sweep things under the rug. In fact she barely swept at all. I minded at first, but I got used to it.

The years with the new people have passed...close to 45 of them. The old dogs left and new ones came. Now there is only one smaller dog; he spends days with me and nights and weekends with the neighbors down the street. The children grew up and went away. They come back sometimes with little people that seem to belong to them. Five little people where there used to be three. They often bring dogs with them as well. And extra friends. My total size has not increased in many years, but I flex more easily and find that I have ample room for everyone who comes. We all fit. I like the noise and laughter.

Music still fills up my space. HE plays the piano every day. He has gotten much better! And there are still a lot of guests who come and go. THEY have never stopped making changes, even though they have not expanded my walls. They installed a pump downstairs, so there is never any water seeping into the basement now. And they turned part of the garage where her car used to go into another sleeping space. There is a nice window, and they put in heat and a rug and a trundle bed. It is surprisingly pleasant and cozy. Returning children and even grown up guests stay there, but I hear THEM saying that they might find someone to come live down there and help them out so they won't have to move. This puzzles me. Why would they make all these changes in me and then move away?

The Walk Back

Walking up the hill, I'm glad I wore my boots. The snow that came down yesterday has turned to gray slush, and the grass is trying for spring. I see it beginning to reach up from the puddled earth.

Jimmy stops to sniff at the edge of the woods. He's checking his messages, as dogs do. I wonder who was there: squirrel, cat, raccoon, coyote? He lifts his leg and leaves his own mark. We make our way up the hill slowly, stopping often for messages. I have the luxury of time today. We both revel in it. The walk is dense with life.

We reach the field. The sky is that deep shade of blue that holds no space for clouds. Never has. I remember discovering the shade when I was a little girl, and I look up now, with an old joy, knowing in a glance that the blue will be unbroken.

We pass through the flat muddy field toward the river and the meadow. As we come to the river path, I notice that the water in the channel is moving, though there are still big patches of ice that look almost safe. For a moment I am back thirty years ago when our black Labrador, Firmly Jones, and his dumb blonde buddy lab, Miss Muffet, raced bravely out on the icy river. Muffet, less willful, responded to our whistle. But Firmly Jones continued and fell through the ice. He screamed. His terror pierced the air. I had never heard a dog scream. I shudder even now, standing on firm ground, hearing that sound again. The story ended well. The dog and his teen-aged rescuer made it to safety. But his cry is etched in my memory

Jimmy and I walk on into the meadow. The sky is still that shade of blue; the trees my sons climbed are thirty-five years taller. So are the sons. The tall grasses that hid them in our games of hide and seek are matted down for winter, waiting for the warmer days to come and games to resume. The pussy willow sprouts little promises that will be buds. I break forsythia branches to bring home and force the spring into coming.

While Jimmy sniffs, I sit on a bench. The sun feels warm on my back. Sometimes I have read there. Mostly I've just been still and caught up on my staring. I remember when the bench came, the winter of 1990, soon after the death of our young friend Suzanne. We planted bulbs around it. They spread and multiplied, and each spring we remember. The metal disc on it does not give the date, just the words, "In loving memory of Suzanne." And for this moment her dark eyes and quick smile flash into my head.

We walk farther into the field. It is quiet and over grown now in its status as conservation land. But for people who know where to look, it still shows traces of a former life. For more than half of the last century in this very spot, the Norumbega Amusement Park swelled with music and carnival rides and a penny arcade. The great swing bands - Benny Goodman, Tommy Dorsey and Artie Shaw - all played here at the Totem Pole. Frank Sinatra and Dinah Shore sang for the dancing crowd that came out from Boston by canoe or trolley. Down by the river there remain some small hooks from the moorings for several hundred canoes that plied their way out from Boston. There are cracked remnants of once paved walks that ran through the lush flower gardens. At the top of one hill we stop at the concrete footings, which are all that remain of a giant Ferris wheel. Jimmy sniffs his way around the edge in hope that recent picnickers may have dropped leftovers. I grab his collar before he can race down to the water for a dip.

The sun feels warm as we walk out into the meadow. At the far end looms a massive beech tree, its trunk looking like an enormous elephant's foot, complete with toes. Well over 40 feet tall, it is climbed only occasionally now by a professional with ropes. He reports carvings with dates as early as 1932 in its upper reaches. Jimmy and I walk there often. Sometimes the three young brothers: Rob, Jack and Max come along with us on their way to the school bus. If all four of us hold hands, we can just barely circle the tree. They call it the Money Tree and look for pennies and the occasional dime in its knotholes. No one knows that I slip in alone to maintain the supply. Their mother shakes her head and says she keeps telling them that money doesn't grow on trees. Then they laugh and open their fists to show her that sometimes it does.

Walking out of the field, we come to the Lyons Little League Park. My sons and their friends played ball here, as had generations before them. The field is fenced now and just a few years ago the younger generation managed to add lights and hot dogs to the area, which has heard so many cheers as bat struck ball. Jimmy catches the scent of a ball and runs in wide to wider circles until he finds one and brings it back triumphantly. I throw it down the path that continues down to the cove. It is quiet here. The leaves are not yet budding, nor have the swans returned. There is still some ice, too thin to bear our weight safely. We stop at a bench. While Jimmy sniffs, I run my hand over the plaque placed here in memory of our friend Steve. His house is directly across the water and the writing acknowledges " A Life Lived Along This River." Our sons grew up together, fishing and skating in this very place. I remind myself to bring clippers to prune back the bushes next time so that his family will be able to see the bench clearly. Steve's absence remains very present. He was a good man who did good things.

We walk back more slowly, the dog and I. The blue of the sky has lightened, and puffy clouds are scudding in. The yellow school bus turns up our street to gather the current batch of children. I wave, and Jimmy wags. We head for home.

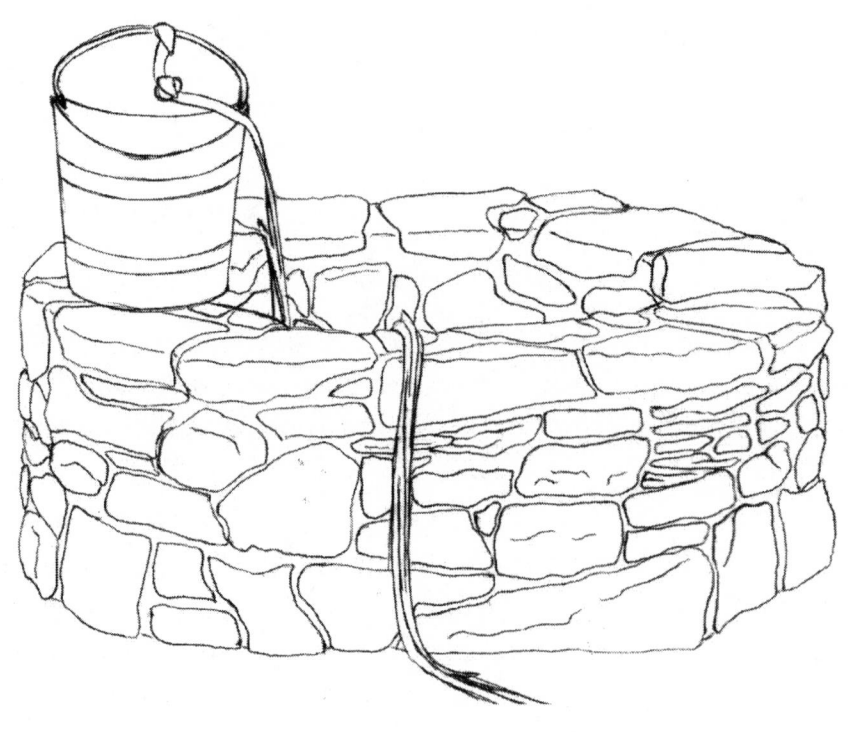

The Well

We don't go to the well any more. Water is piped directly into our homes, iced or instantly hot. Programmed sprinklers soak our lawns, two hours before sunrise and one hour after sunset, even if it is raining. We humidify in winter and dehumidify in summer. All the water we need runs right to us, and so we have no need to go to the well.

We don't gather at the river either. We haven't gone there to wash clothes for over a hundred years. We have washing machines and convenience stores. No more stopping at the green grocer or the fishmonger or even the hardware store. They are gone. Replaced by malls and marts where we get more for less – and faster. We're new and improved, with twenty-five hours for the price of twenty-four.

So who misses the well? It was not so great. You had to walk a ways just to get there, and then wait in line. Sometimes the water had bugs in it, and folks got sick. Even at best, the pails were heavy, and the water sloshed over as you carried it home. And then you had to do it all over again tomorrow.

Maybe that's the point. You had to go get it all over again the next day, and so did everyone else. As you walked along, maybe you thought about the day ahead and the day just behind. These days were relentlessly similar. You noticed that the brown field on your left was beginning to green up. You wondered if old Mr. Thomas had died in the night. He'd been sick for months. His son Ted sold their produce in the Friday market now. His granddaughter Emily, just seven years old, came along. She was learning to make change, so you had to wait while she counted. You knew she'd get better quickly. She was a bright little girl.

You saw the boy from way across town jump and touch a branch, and you realized how tall he had grown. You told his little brother to come down out of the beech tree on the edge of the woods because he had climbed too high. You noticed the fifteen year old girl-turning-woman who never used to come to the well. She too had grown tall, and her chestnut hair was glossy. She turned up every day now, just about the time the young carpenter passed by.

You thought of your own son and remembered how proud he had been the year he was big enough to go to the well and bring the water home by himself. He was a man now, and the bright eyes and ready smile were gone. The foreman on his work crew turned away when you greeted him last week so you couldn't look him in the eye. Perhaps he knew you were afraid for your boy and hoped that life might yet deal more kindly with him. You reached the well and spoke of these thoughts—or kept silent and just brought the water home. There would be time to speak tomorrow to whoever might be there.

It was hard and sometimes cold, fetching water—always tiring, and relentlessly routine. Surely none of us would go back to this. Who would choose the well over instant hot water and press-button ice cubes? Or the riverbank over the Maytag? Aren't we better off?

Perhaps. Certainly, in some ways. But haven't we lost something? A year or two ago a new family moved into the Chapman's house on our street. They were a young couple with a small boy and a dog. She works nights as a nurse; he works days at home doing something with computers. They keep the place up and are quiet. We say a pleasant hello whenever we pass on the street or meet in the grocery store.

One evening our computer went down. We needed to get something out before tomorrow, and we thought the problem might be simple to fix. We were still making friends with our computer. Maybe the new guy in the Chapman's house could help us.

Since we didn't really know them well enough to walk up to their door and ask, we decided to phone. That way we could identify ourselves. We had the Chapman's number on the Rolodex, but of course it was disconnected. We realized that we didn't know the last name of the new people, so we called around the neighborhood. No one knew. "Oh, that pleasant couple in the Chapman's house?" said their neighbor three doors down. "His name is Don, I think. Cute little kid. Good about keeping that dog of theirs on a leash. No, we don't know their last name. How long have they been here? Couple of years?"

Six calls later, we still had no name for the folks in the Chapman house.

Wait a minute! What's wrong here? Well, for one thing, it isn't the Chapman's house anymore. The Chapmans moved away, and the Somebodys bought that house. They have a child and a dog and their own hopes and dreams. They live in *their* house, not the Chapman's house. They live right up the street from us, and we haven't any idea who they are. We've been remiss.

But then again, maybe it's not so bad. We live comfortably. The water comes. The lights work. Satellites bounce the news right into our eyes and ears and iPhones. We know what is happening on Wall Street and in Syria. We check Facebook often enough. Is the name of our neighbors important? They might be boring. Or meddlesome. Or needy.

Before we know it, that sweet small boy will be playing music at screeching volume and smoking and drinking with his buddies in the park at the top of the hill. Maybe we don't need to know the folks in the Chapman house after all.

We've moved into fast forward and lost the sense of community that made the trip worthwhile. Our social contract has no social contact. We connect on line, but we no longer speak to each other. We don't know Mr. Thomas, so how can we care that he might have died? We do not recognize the boy who climbed too high in the tree, so we don't call him to come down to a safer spot.

Even though we don't need the water, we need to find another way to go to the well.

Epilogue

This collection has been a walk through a period of time in the century just ended, as well as a glimpse into the one now begun. It is seen first through the eyes of a little girl growing up in a strong family during troubled times in the deeply segregated South. In addition the news of World War II was broadcast daily on the yellow-eyed radio. It was a time of ration coupons, paper drives, and black out drills with heavy green shades. I was that little girl, and I have been blessed with a chance to reflect and write as the next century moves forward. It is a kind of double vision. I am fortunate indeed to have clear memories of childhood, though I have come to realize that memory can be a trickster. The events of that time remain the same in hindsight, but my understanding of them has grown more complex and subtle, and perhaps thereby more fair. I recall being puzzled when my mother wept at news that the war had ended. I had never known a world without war, and I had never experienced or seen tears of joy. Awareness of contradictions in life thus began early. The nature of humans is that we live life forward, and make sense of it backward.

Often that sense comes through in the recounting of events through stories…a practice common in the South.

When friends have asked, "Why are you doing this writing? " I have not always had a ready answer, except to echo Socrates, who is credited with saying that the unexamined life is not worth living. Looking again at my life from a distance has offered deeper insights, expanding my heart and mind as I find a bigger and more complex picture of a world gone by. As I understand more, I find that I am inclined to judge less. I also take advantage of this opportunity to offer in the last stories a few thoughts about the days we now inhabit. Many of us seem hard-wired to try to make sense of our life experience if we have the privilege of time and the capacity to do so. In this, as in many other ways, I have been fortunate. I am keenly aware of the richness of my life and I am grateful to have walked the earth in good company.

So, what matters? What are the rewards of gathering the account of a life? First, the realization that no account can be considered "the whole truth." Truth lies in the selected and edited observations of the beholder, and it can be a slippery beast. But the benchmarks did indeed occur. World War II came to a close, only to be followed by other wars in my young years. The fighting continued in Korea. General Douglas MacArthur was my hero, and I was baffled when President Truman called him home. My sister Meg and I kept a MacArthur classic comic book on the table between our beds. The Arab/Israeli conflict filled the news then and continues to this day. Viet Nam was yet to come.

Jim Crow ended officially, but left a residue of unresolved injustice that continues to crumble all too slowly. Despite electing our first black President in 2008, the country still must travel a long road to achieve equal opportunity regardless of color.

I have benefited from writing this life review. I think particularly of my parents and what a large imprint their life circumstances and their ways of dealing with racial injustice made on their three children. I am keenly aware that hindsight offers 20/20 vision, and that decisions must be made with the information available in the moment one is living. For a considerable time I wished that our parents had told us more, but I have come to realize that they lived their beliefs in a way that made a difference. My siblings and I did not miss that lesson.

Preparing this book has also allowed reflection on my own marriage of over half a century to Frank, and of the immense privilege that we have been given of sharing a life. We rejoice in our three sons formed from the same gene pool, but possessing very individual amalgams of personality and character. They are grown now with sons and nephews of their own, and I hope that life will treat them kindly as their stories continue to unfold. I am proud that like their parents and grandparents, they are all involved in teaching.

I look to the expansion of both wisdom and knowledge, as the world grows smaller. I dare to hope that our capacity for living together, in kindness to each other and to the planet, may grow greater. As the hobbit says, "The road goes ever on."

A Family History

Aura Holton (Betsy's mother; third from left) behind her mother
c. 1915

James Godard (Betsy's father) on his way to College
c. 1920

James Godard, a graduate student at Duke where he met Aura Holton
c. 1925

Aura Godard (left) with baby Meg and her two older cousins
c. 1933

James Godard with baby Meg
c. 1932

Aura Godard outside their home on the Queens College campus
c. 1940

Young Betsy with older brother Jerry
c. 1940

Young Betsy
c. 1942

Betsy and older sister Meg in the North Carolina mountains
c. 1948

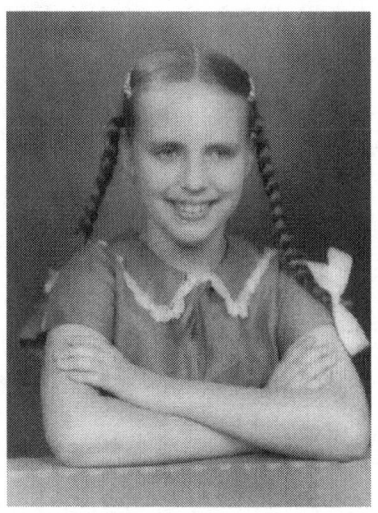

Betsy, Charlotte, North Carolina
1948

Betsy Godard, Coral Gables, Florida
c. 1954

Frank Bunn just before meeting Betsy, Philadelphia, Pennsylvania
c. 1960

Frank Bunn (far left in front) in Fort Knox Kentucky
1966

Betsy and Frank with their parents on their wedding day
June 9, 1962

Betsy in her junior year of college studying abroad in England
c. 1957

Betsy and son Andy with their temporary dog Montfort
c.1973

Son George swinging in Fort Knox, Kentucky
1966

Son Ted at Mary Threadgold's Nursery School
1971

Aura and James outside son Jerry's home in Greensboro
c. 1980

Aura and James with son Jerry and two of his daughters
c. 1980

Aura in a precious moment of clarity in her last years
c. 1981

Frank with grandson Eli
2004

Betsy and Frank
2002

All the grandsons (left to right: Eli, Sam, Micah, Franklin, John
c. 2007

Betsy and grandsons, Lake Michigan
2008

Ted and Ashley
2009

Left to right: Yamilla, Franklin, dog Roscoe, George, John
2014

Top to bottom: Eli, Andy, Micah, Rebecca, Sam
2008

"Never let the truth interfere with art"
- Aura Holton Godard